Human Resource Management in the Public Sector

Edited by
Rona S. Beattie and Stephen P. Osborne

 Routledge
Taylor & Francis Group

LONDON AND NEW YORK

First published 2008 by Routledge
2 Park Square, Milton Park, Abingdon, Oxon, OX14 4RN

Simultaneously published in the USA and Canada
by Routledge
270 Madison Ave, New York NY 10016

Reprinted 2008

Transferred to Digital Printing 2008

Routledge is an imprint of the Taylor & Francis Group, an informa business

© 2008 Rona S. Beattie and Stephen P. Osborne

Typeset in Perpetua by KnowledgeWorks Global Limited, Southampton, Hampshire, UK

British Library Cataloguing in Publication Data
A catalogue record for this book is available from the British Library

Library of Congress Cataloging in Publication Data
A catalog record for this book has been requested

ISBN 10: 0-415-37292-5 (hbk)
ISBN 10: 0-415-46425-0 (pbk)

ISBN 13: 978-0-415-37292-3 (hbk)
ISBN 13: 978-0-415-46425-3 (pbk)

Publisher's Note
The publisher has gone to great lengths to ensure the quality of this reprint but points
out that some imperfections in the original may be apparent

Human Resource Management in the Public Sector

Human Resource Management (HRM) is a core element of any service, but especially so in public service organizations, whose employees are often their most valuable resource. However, until now there has been little information readily available in the form of key texts which explore this important topic. Now, this outstanding book tackles the subject head on, bringing together cutting-edge research on HRM in the public sector from a range of respected international authors. It covers such key issues as:

- the relationship between HRM and organizational performance
- managing cultural change and the work-life balance.

Timely and topical, this key book will be of great interest both to researchers in the fields of HRM and public sector management, and to management practitioners keen to inform their practice from an evidence base.

This book was first published as a special issue of *Public Management Review*.

Rona Beattie is at the Caledonian Business School at Glasgow, Caledonian University.

Stephen Osborne is Professor of International Public Management in the Management School at the University of Edinburgh.

CONTENTS

EDITORIAL

The idea for this special issue emerged from the International Research Symposium in Public Management in Hong Kong where a panel on HRM recognized that scholarly activity investigating HRM in the public sector was relatively underdeveloped compared to work in the corporate sector. This special issue is an attempt to address that deficit. Particularly pleasing is that the articles come from the UK, Europe and Australia, which allows us to explore HRM in a range of contrasting public sector environments.

There are seven excellent articles presented in this issue, several of which were first presented in Hong Kong.

Kerry Brown provides an insightful contextual analysis of HRM in the public sector, which sets the scene for the following six articles, and argues that HRM in the public sector is a major influence in public sector change; a recurring theme in all the articles.

Rodwell and Teo's article provides an interesting comparative analysis between the public and private sectors within health care in Australia. A key conclusion emerging from their study is the contribution of human capital enhancing HR practices to organizational performance, and of the need for HR specialists to adopt a change agent role in collaboration with senior management colleagues. Thus they provide further evidence of the growing strategic importance of HRM.

Méhaut and Perez also provide a comparative analysis between the public and private sector, in this case the provision of further education and training; a key aspect of French public policy given the mandatory requirement on employers to invest a percentage of their total wage bill on training. Here they conclude that Human Resource Development is not sufficiently strategic, evidenced by the lack of HRD representation on the top executive team, which is then mirrored by lack of middle management commitment; often the pivotal stakeholder in the implementation of HRD initiatives.

Waterhouse and Lewis's article explores the relationship between communication and change in a large public sector department and the implications for HRM emerging from that interaction. A key conclusion emerging from their article, contrary to much of the normative literature, is that it is perhaps inappropriate to try and create mono-cultures in large organizations and that it might be more effective to manage the communication channels between the disparate sub-cultures, that inevitably exist, to ensure they understand how their roles contribute to the overall strategy of the organization.

Maxwell and McDougall's article focuses on work–life balance, an area of HRM that has been significantly impacted on by government policy and changes in employment law. The UK Prime Minister and Chancellor of the Exchequer both acted as role models in this field, taking paternity leave following the births of their children. This article explores the different levels of influence on work–life balance developments including macro, organizational and individual factors. Their empirical work focuses on voluntary and public service organizations in Scotland. A key conclusion from their study was that the organizations reported that there had been very positive effects from work–life balance policies and practices. There are therefore important lessons for other voluntary and public sector employers emerging from their work, in particular the critical role that line managers play in implementing such policies; a recurring theme in this special issue.

Butterfield, Edwards and Woodall's article also develops the role of operational line managers, in this case the role of police sergeants within a major UK police force; an organization often difficult for scholars to get research access to. Their focus is on the implementation of performance management as part of the parcel of New Public Management policies affecting the police service. A key conclusion emerging from this study was the role conflict and strain facing the sergeants who still undertook an operational role while being required to undertake additional managerial duties such as performance appraisal; an experience being increasingly shared by line managers across sectors as a result of the increasing devolution of HR operational responsibilities. They also found that much of the rhetoric of New Public Management was not realized in practice.

The final article in this special issue focuses on partnership working, an important element of the Government's 'Third Way' policy for the delivery of public services in the UK. Mann, Pritchard and Rummery focus on partnership working within the health and social care sector and investigate a particular aspect of partnership working that is often neglected by policy makers, namely the need to develop the partnership and the key players within it. Absolutely vital in partnership development is the development of trust between partners that often emerges from the experience of working successfully together and overcoming interprofessional mistrust, which often results from mutual ignorance. They explore these issues by examining the contribution of action learning processes to partnership working.

This special issue has revealed both similarities and differences between public and private sector practice of HRM. In particular it demonstrates how HRM in the public sector has been influenced by government policy. It is hoped that this special issue has met its primary objective, which was to stimulate debate about the nature and practice of HRM in the public sector across international boundaries, and that it will encourage HRM and public management scholars to continue to explore this increasingly important subject.

As well as thanking all the above authors for their contributions to this special issue I would also like to thank the reviewers from the UK, USA, Europe and Australia who took the time and effort to review thoroughly all submissions for this special edition. I would also like to thank Professor Stephen Osborne, the journal's Editor-in-Chief for giving me the opportunity to edit this special issue. Finally, thanks to Hannah Clement for her editorial support. As always any errors are mine alone.

Rona S. Beattie

Caledonian Business School Glasgow Caledonian University Scotland

HUMAN RESOURCE MANAGEMENT IN THE PUBLIC SECTOR

Kerry Brown

INTRODUCTION

This overview of Human Resource Management (HRM) in the public sector establishes that HRM is a major influence in public sector change. The bureaucratic and the management models of public sector operation and activity are compared to discern the ways in which employment and organizational issues are conceptualized in each model. The manner in which the institutional, policy and organizational changes impact public sector employment and conditions of service is explored.

While changes to the public sector over the past two decades have had a significant impact on employees of public sector organizations and the conditions under which people work, there has been scant attention afforded to the specific field of Human Resource Management research and academic inquiry in relation to the public sector. Moreover, contemporary HRM texts often disregard or give only cursory acknowledgement of HRM within the public sector, relying instead on appropriating a business model of firms as the general context for HRM scholarship.

The article begins by defining and detailing the scope and features of HRM. The article proceeds by describing and examining the traditional model of public administration and then moves on to consider the place and function of personnel within this bureaucratic model. The emergence of the contemporary model of public management is traced to demonstrate the scope and character of public sector reform. The articulation of HRM and public management accords with efforts to develop a systematic response to reform and restructuring initiatives in the public sector through achieving greater staff and operational efficiencies together with cutbacks to government expenditure. The applicability of HRM to the public sector is examined and discussed.

HUMAN RESOURCE MANAGEMENT

Human Resource Management has as its central focus, 'managing people within the employer – employee relationship' and involves marshalling the productive capacity of an organization's members (Stone 1995: 4). Stone suggests the domain of HRM covers the 'acquisition, development, reward and motivation maintenance and departure' (1995: 10 – 13) of employees and typical areas of concern include HR planning and capability audits, recruitment and selection of employees, skill development and training, career progression, performance appraisal, formulating employment conditions and compensation and reward. Further, Wright and Ferris (1996) add that HRM is concerned with understanding and interpreting the legal framework and context regulating conditions of employment and employment relations.

In addition, however, effective Human Resource Management is argued to deliver competitive advantage to firms (Walker 1992). The ability to achieve this advantage in a rapidly changing and dynamic environment has further extended the focus of HRM to include developing organizational capacity to adapt to changing environmental contingencies (Wright and Snell 1998). In this way, the effective deployment and management of people within organizations is purported to be a powerful tool to respond to complex and turbulent environments and achieve superior organizational outcomes.

The applicability of HRM to public sector organizations, then, is clearly established. Public sector organizations need to hire, develop and train employees, and establish payment systems, set conditions of employment and develop a coherent set of employment policies. However, the particularity of the public sector with a focus on public interest outcomes rather than private interests may add a layer of complexity that does not easily fit with HRM as a strategic partner in achieving organizational competitiveness and business outcomes.

A traditional model of the public sector

The application of HRM principles within the public sector displaced the traditional model of personnel administration. HRM in the public sector was argued to have been introduced when the sector experienced a shift from a 'rule-bound' culture to a 'performance-based' culture (Shim 2001). The adoption of HRM paralleled the extensive public sector managerial restructuring and reform programme. Managerial objectives of greater efficiencies are argued to be achieved through effective human resource practices offered by adopting HRM principles (Kramar 1986). The adoption of New Public Management (NPM) then may have opened the possibility of managers acquiring or developing sophisticated HRM techniques. Thus, NPM principles allow a more flexible and responsive approach to questions of recruitment, selection, retention, training and development of public sector employees.

The public sector developed a distinctive approach to HRM over time and featured many innovations that delivered significant rights and entitlements to employees. The public sector has been perceived as the 'model employer' and conditions of service have been at the forefront of employment reform and innovation. The notion of the model employer encapsulated the principles of best practice and was argued to set an example to the private sector in terms of fair treatment of employees and providing good conditions of service including high levels of job security, superior leave entitlements and generous pensions (Black and Upchurch 1999: 506).

In the traditional model of the public sector, a bureaucratic employment policy matched the operation of Weberian practices and principles of rule-governed rational action. The administrative system was subjected to a bureaucratization of procedures to ensure that decisions and actions were consistent, formalized and systematically addressed activities through a pre-defined application of rules and processes. Aspects of a rational-legal bureaucracy that reflected concern with employees and their administration included specialization through functional responsibility, formalized rules to prevent arbitrary dismissal, a reliance on organizational position to confer authority, selection by merit and, generally, a career service (Schroeder 1992).

In this setting, the employment system was highly centralized and run by powerful central agencies that were responsible for all the hire decisions, setting establishment numbers and formulating rules for employment, training and career development (Alford 1993). Employment in the public sector was based on the notion of a 'career service' of security of tenure and lifelong employment and was framed through the operation of an internal labour market (Gardner and Palmer 1997). Employees were recruited to the public service at the lower ranks of departments and promotion to higher-level positions was restricted to internal public sector applicants, unless the position was highly specialized.

The public sector had service-wide remuneration and conditions, so that variation on the basis of performance was not allowed; payment was based on the job or position. Job positions were narrow, specific task-based and highly routinized, and administration was developed according to Tayloristic work practices of separating constituent elements of work to achieve economies of scale. Strict seniority or length of service was the basis for promotion.

This unitary system came under pressure through financial crisis and a keenness for governments to contract their services amid mounting criticism of 'big government' (Shim 2001). The demands for a new approach to management that allowed greater flexibility in dealing with staff issues were based in the rhetoric of the need for greater responsiveness and efficiency.

A new model of public management

The introduction of New Public Management with an emphasis on transferring private sector management techniques into the public sector shifted the emphasis in the public sector from administration to management and was part of a broad strategy to achieve efficiency, effectiveness and quality of service. Changes to the public sector were introduced in response to the perceived need to reduce government expenditure, provide more efficient services and decrease the scope and reach of government-provided public goods and services (Weller 1996: 2). Elements of NPM included managing for results, performance measurement, corporate planning, user pays, devolution of authority, decentralization of activities and risk management.

Managerialism under a NPM model involved the application of physical, financial and human resources to realize government objectives. The new model of public management is argued to be a 'flexible, market-based form' (Hughes 1994: 1). The rhetoric of New Public Management denoted it as the 'arts of private sector management' extended into the public sector (Gray and Jenkins 1995: 80). These new business practices also embraced new ways of managing public sector employees. Thus human resource management was included in the public sector reform agenda.

Traditional notions of a career service, stable and lifelong employment and service-wide employment conditions were challenged by New Public Management principles and practices.

HRM in the public sector

Public sector HRM has been characterized by the creation of more flexible structures and processes, the removal of highly centralized agencies and service-wide consistency of rules and greater responsibility accorded to line managers and supervisors in the management of employees through flatter management structures and programmes of decentralization and devolution (Gardner 1993; Gardner and Palmer 1997; Shim 2001). At the job level, broader and multi-skilled jobs were introduced. There was also a greater concentration on performance and output measures.

The new models of HRM in the public sector introduced the notion of human resources having the capacity to achieve performance outcomes in line with the strategic direction of the public sector organization (Gardner and Palmer 1997). With this orientation, there was an emphasis on securing and retaining staff who could achieve desired outcomes and, along with this focus, a dismantling of the internal labour market and little or no commitment to maintaining job security. The human resource system relied on performance management for workforce flexibility and productivity.

The new system however, has been criticized for the resultant erosion of employment conditions and opportunities for career development. Large-scale downsizing and contracting out has also arguably contributed to poorer quality of service delivery. With the major changes and reforms to the public sector under NPM, there has been a dilution of some of the practices and conditions that have traditionally set the public sector apart from other organizations in the private and non-profit sectors. The consequences of adopting NPM practices and principles were argued to have meant a cutting back of employees' benefits and wages, staff reductions and changes in organizational culture and structure (Black and Upchurch 1999).

It is also clear that the reforms have driven changes in the way the public sector interacts with and shapes relations with external organizations. Contracting out and competitive tendering have delivered new models of market-based service delivery (Klijn 2002). Accordingly, the changing nature of government delivery of services has altered the nature of relations between the public sector and other sectors, particularly the community sector. Greater competition between service delivery organizations and contracting out have pressured community sector organizations to respond to broader types of service delivery under conditions of competitive tendering or through contractual arrangements that specify more closely the way the human resources are deployed to deliver services. This has meant greater expectations on the part of government funding bodies in relation to community organizations for ensuring better structural organization and more skilled human resources to deliver services (Brown and Ryan 2003).

The changing dimensions of public sector employment indicate that HRM has had a major impact on the operation of the public sector. The contribution of human resource management to understanding the constituent elements of the 'new' public sector is significant. New Public Management has a place on centre stage in terms of affecting the agenda for change. Multiskilling, restructured career paths, abolition of seniority as a basis for promotion, greater emphasis on equity considerations and the removal of rigid employment categories have been some of the benefits of shifting from personnel administration to HRM in the public sector (Brown 1997).

Emerging new concerns in relation to new directions and approaches for HRM in the public sector centre on the organizational effects of ever-increasing levels of technology, changes in population patterns affecting labour markets and new demands on management leadership. Areas of emerging concern and challenge to HRM in the public sector are the advances being made possible by highly sophisticated information technology including human resource information systems, the importance of understanding the implications of demographic trends such as the ageing population, the need for additional attention to leadership and leadership development and the greater emphasis on workforce capability and systems of knowledge management (Shim 2001). The different orientation of the public sector from the for-profit, private sector means that while HRM has commonalities across all sectors in its attention to workforce issues, HRM in the public sector will exhibit a range of differences to that of private sector HRM.

CONCLUSION

The problems besetting the public sector that ushered in NPM required more than simply maintaining a traditional context for bureaucratic action. Rising costs and the need for fiscal restraint, a loss of community confidence in the ability of government to be responsive to the community and structural change drove government and public sector leaders to seek a radically different model for operating and structuring the public sector.

The more pertinent question relates not to how appropriate is the general thrust of reform that transposes business criteria onto the delivery of public services, but what is the relevant reform direction given prevailing public sector conditions and context. Calculations about HRM as a key platform for reform can then be usefully undertaken. What is at stake is the balance between competing values about the role and purpose of the public sector and the possibility of recuperating a viable human resource model that considers both the particular character of the public service and also responds to the shifting conditions wrought by new management practices.

REFERENCES

Alford, J. (1993) 'Thinking About the Demise of Public Service Boards in Commonwealth and State Government' in M. Gardner (ed.) *Human Resource Management and Industrial Relations in the Public Sector.* Melbourne: Macmillan.

Black, J. and Upchurch, M. (1999) 'Public Sector Employment' in G. Hollinshead, P. Nicholls and S. Tailby (eds) *Employee Relations.* London: Financial Times Management.

Brown, K. (1997) 'Evaluating Equity Outcomes in State Public Sectors: A Comparison of Three Housing Agencies'. *Australian Journal of Public Administration*, 56:4 pp57 – 66.

Brown, K. and Ryan, N. (2003) 'Redefining Government – Community Relations through Service Agreements'. *Journal of Contemporary Issues in Business and Government*, 9:1 pp21 – 30.

Gardner, M. (1993) 'Introduction' in M. Gardner (ed.) *Human Resource Management and Industrial Relations in the Public Sector.* Melbourne: Macmillan.

Gardner, M. and Palmer, G. (1997) *Employment Relations: Industrial Relations and Human Resource Management in Australia* (2nd edn), Melbourne: Macmillan.

Gray, A. and Jenkins, B. (1995) 'From Public Administration to Public Management: Reassessing a Revolution'. *Public Administration*, 73:1 pp75 – 99.

Hughes, O. (1994) *Public Management and Administration*, London: St Martin's Press.

Klijn, H.-E. (2002) 'Governing Networks in the Hollow State: Contracting Out, Process Management or a Combination of the Two?'. *Public Management Review*, 4:2 pp149 – 65.

Kramar, R. (1986) 'The Personnel Practitioner and Affirmative Action', *Human Resource Management Australia*, 24:1 pp 38 – 44.

Schroeder, R. (1992) *Max Weber and the Sociology of Culture*, London: Sage Publications.

Shim, D. (2001) 'Recent Human Resources Developments in OECD Member Countries'. *Public Personnel Management*, 30:3 pp323 – 47.

Stone, R. (1995) *Human Resource Management*, Brisbane: Wiley.

Walker, J. W. (1992) *Human Resource Strategy*, New York: McGraw-Hill.

Weller, P. (1996) 'The Universality of Public Sector Reform' in P. Weller and G. Davis (eds) *New Ideas, Better Government*. Sydney: Allen & Unwin.

Wright, P. and Snell, S. (1998) 'Toward a Unifying Framework for Exploring Fit and Flexibility in Strategic Human Resource Management', *Academy of Management Journal*, 23:4 pp756 – 73.

Wright, P. and Ferris, G. (1996) 'Human Resources Management: Past, Present and Future' in G. Ferris and M. Buckley (eds) *Human Resources Management: Perspectives, Context, Functions, and Outcomes* (3rd edn). New Jersey: Prentice-Hall.

STRATEGIC HRM IN FOR-PROFIT AND NON-PROFIT ORGANIZATIONS IN A KNOWLEDGE-INTENSIVE INDUSTRY

The same issues predict performance for both types of organization

John J. Rodwell and Stephen T. T. Teo

Private sector firms have often emphasized the importance of leveraging knowledge to create core capabilities and achieve competitive advantage (Zack 1999). One of the key means of creating these capabilities is through using strategic Human Resource Management (HRM) to manage firm performance in knowledge-based firms (e.g. Wright et al. 2001a). The public and non-profit sector has often received comment about their bureaucratic personnel management system, with differences found in terms of the adoption of HRM between public and private sector firms (Boyne et al. 1999). Is strategic HRM evident in public and non-profit organizations? If so, how successful have the public and non-profit sector been in using knowledge-oriented practices to manage performance in knowledge-based firms?

Health services and professional medical services are a key knowledge-based industry in the public and non-profit sector. These medical organizations employ individuals who are highly skilled, and produce, distribute and use knowledge and information as their source of competitive advantage (OECD 1996). The Australian health industry is complex, with private, public and non-public sector provision of health services and over the last decade there has been an increase in the corporatization of health care services, including private health care services (AIHW 2002). According to a recent report by the Australian Institute of Health and Welfare (AIHW 2003), the industry employed a total of 405,250 individuals in health occupations (such as medical practitioners, nurses, dentists and other allied health workers) in 2001. The Australian health sector experienced an increase in the number of people employed in the 2001 – 2 period, an increase from 8 to 10 per cent of GDP (ABS 2003) and it represents the fourth largest employing industry division in the Australian economy (AIHW 2003).

Health services (HS) organizations in the for-profit and non-profit sector are undergoing widespread transformations (Russell et al. 1999; Narine and Persaud 2003). On-going reforms in the hospital sector affect organizational structures, the adoption of total quality management and result in changes in the management of hospitals and patients and the ways in which hospitals are funded (Braithwaite 1993; Narine and Persaud 2003). The HS organizations of the future will have little resemblance to their predecessors, due to the reform of health care policies in countries such as Australia (e.g. Boldy et al. 1996; European Observatory on Health Care Systems 2001), the UK and the USA (Boldy et al. 1996; Russell et al. 1999).

According to Russell and his colleagues (1999), due to the inefficiencies in the health sector world-wide, reform in the health sector has been linked to public sector reform and ideas and initiatives, such as that of 'New Public Management' (NPM). Some examples of these changes include the development of internal competition through separating purchaser and provider activities, undertaken payment reform and the contracting of clinical and non-clinical staff. There is also an increasing emphasis on the adoption of private sector HRM practices and decentralization of HRM to line managers (Thompson et al. 1999).

Human resource (HR) issues in the health services sector have often been acknowledged as important (Barnett *et al.* 1996; Thompson *et al.* 1999; Rondeau and Wagar 2001; Truss 2003) and HR practices are also the primary mechanism for developing human capital (Becker 1993). However, little is known of the extent to which HRM is being managed in the non-profit sector (Bach 2000; Rondeau and Wagar 2001).

Together, the use of HR practices as a mechanism for leveraging knowledge highlights the need for more research on the management of knowledge workers in medical organizations, particularly those in the public and non-profit sector. Therefore, the main aim of the current study is to address these gaps in the literature by examining the relationships between the nature and orientation of the HRM systems and performance, for both for-profit and non-profit organizations in the Australian health services industry and thereby increase our understanding of the nature of HRM in the public and non-profit sector.

The structure of the article is as follows. The next sections explore the extent to which the adoption of strategic HRM by Australian HS firms enhances firm performance. The first issue of interest is to examine the impact of external and internal orientation on the adoption of strategic HRM and firm performance. The second issue of interest is to examine whether there are any similarities and differences in the adoption of strategic HRM between profit and non-profit HS firms. The remaining sections then review the method, the statistics used and the results. The theoretical and practical implications of the results are then discussed.

KNOWLEDGE WORKERS AND STRATEGIC HRM IN HEALTH SERVICE FIRMS

Knowledge workers and firm performance

Globalization and technological developments in new information and communication technologies have made intangible assets a relatively important source of competitive advantage for knowledge-based firms (OECD 1996; Teece 1998), when compared to the more traditional sources of advantage such as product and process technology, protected or regulated markets, access to financial resources and economies of scale (Vicere 2000). The importance of conceptualizing firms as heterogeneous, knowledge-bearing entities can be found in the strategic management literature (Hoskisson *et al.* 1999). The knowledge-based view of the firm postulates that knowledge is the only resource that provides sustainable competitive advantage, and therefore, the firm's attention and decision making should focus primarily on knowledge and the competitive capabilities derived from it (Roberts 2000). Firm capabilities (including core competencies) should then be developed to create knowledge that satisfies the criterion of being a scarce resource, in order to sustain competitive advantage (Snell *et al.* 1996; Storey and Quintas 2001).

The importance of intangibles has brought about an increasing emphasis on treating HR as an organization's most important asset (Snell *et al*. 1996; Barney and Wright 1998). Subsequently, a strategic approach to HRM is able to provide a source of competitive advantage for firms by developing a set of complementary practices that develop employee skills and motivation towards the attainment of the firm's goals and strategies through building intangible assets.

Over the last ten years there has been an increasing interest in the theoretical underpinnings of strategic HRM, with a particular focus on HRM's contribution to firm performance (e.g. Huselid 1995; Wright *et al*. 2001a). These studies highlight two of the major characteristics of strategic HRM: (1) the linkage between HR and business strategies (e.g. Schuler 1992); and (2) HRM's positive relationship with firm performance (e.g. Huselid 1995; Becker and Huselid 1998). Evidence of the benefits of strategic HRM could encourage for-profit and non-profit firms to adopt such an approach (Guthrie 2001).

Strategic HRM and organizational orientation

The adoption of New Public Management practices as part of public sector reform has a number of organizational consequences such as a renewed emphasis on accountability in public policy programmes (Ryan 1993) and a creation of an entrepreneurial spirit among managers (Aulich *et al*. 2001). This has resulted in a shift in organizational orientation from one that is inwardly focused to one that focuses on the external environment (Parker and Bradley 2000). Similarly, a feature of a strategic approach to HRM requires an alignment between the firm's external and internal structures (e.g. Beer *et al*. 1984; Schuler 1992). From a knowledge management perspective, the strength of both the internal and external orientation mechanisms within the firm can often provide a context for the development of human capital-enhancing activities (e.g. see Sveiby 1997). Similarly, organizations in the HS industry may have varying degrees of commercialization, due to unique factors associated with that organization and not just whether the organization is for-profit or non-profit. Subsequently, to investigate the impact of the orientation of the firm on their strategic HRM this study will explore key aspects of both external and internal orientation.

External orientation

Within knowledge management, the relationships the organization has with customers and suppliers, as well as its brand, are facets of the organization's externally oriented intangible assets (Sveiby 1997). The level of the customers' requirements for product performance and the sophistication of their technical standards and specifications is a key stimulus for the development of intangible assets. When customers become more demanding they prompt firms to learn specific customer needs and develop products of superior value (Wheelwright and Clark 1992). That is, one of the core elements for building intangible assets is the degree of Customer Demandingness (Li and Calantone 1998).

Organizations with very demanding customers are challenged to address those demands, thereby creating new processes, new answers and new products, or, at the least, applying or expanding the organization's current state of knowledge and understanding of their customers. Subsequently, organizations in the same industry that have customers of varying degrees of demandingness could develop differing levels of knowledge between the organizations.

From a HRM perspective, strategic HRM should be considered as a service function (Schneider 1994) and subsequently would reflect an external orientation. For example, the HRM function has also been urged to become customer-oriented by involving customers in its systems (Ulrich 1992).

Conversely, having a market orientation has been found to have an influence on the foundation of organizational learning (Slater and Narver 1995), essential for developing a strategic HRM orientation. Ewing et al. (1999) found that organizations that possess a higher level of market orientation have a more effective HRM function. Hence, it is expected that the more Customer Demandingness possessed by an organization, the more likely it is the organization is going to adopt strategic HRM as a means of enhancing organizational effectiveness.

Hypothesis 1: Customer Demandingness is positively related to the adoption of strategic HRM in health services firms.

Internal orientation

The know-how of employees and the culture of the firm, among other factors, are critical in ensuring that the intangible resources of the firm (such as the skills, abilities and capabilities of its employees) are managed strategically to achieve competitive advantage (Hall 1993). An organization's commitment to its employees reflects the firm's focus on investing in competence development (Lee and Miller 1999). Perceived Organizational Commitment to Employees (OCE) engenders a sense of involvement with the company and greater employee initiative and innovation, independent of direct rewards (Shore and Wayne 1993). Hence, it is hypothesized that firms that possess a higher level of OCE will result in adopting a more strategic HRM orientation towards their employees.

Hypothesis 2: Perceived OCE is positively related to the adoption of strategic HRM in health services firms.

Strategic HRM and human capital-enhancing HR practices

From a knowledge management perspective, there is a relationship between a firm's intangible resources and its HR, because strategic people management practices can be used to enhance the individual competence of the firm's employees (Sveiby 1997). Although an organization has little control over the intangible assets that constitute its external structure, the largest and most central form of intangible assets is human capital (Snell and Dean 1992) and there is widespread recognition that these intangibles reside within a resource that the organization does have some control over — the firm's employees (Barney and Wright 1998). The internal aspects of the firm such as skills, experience and knowledge are known as human capital (Parnes 1984; Davenport 1999), which contribute to the value of the firm (Schultz 1961; Becker 1993).

The volatility of the health industry environment also requires the internal operations of a firm to be flexible (EOHCS 2001). HS firms face a number of pressures in the business environment, such as health care funding and the need to achieve flexible organizational structures. This has created an increasing emphasis on a flexible workforce. Indeed, the importance of HR practices in the management of knowledge workers cannot be underestimated (Storey and Quintas 2001). With an increasing focus on the management of knowledge workers as a source of competitive advantage, the human capital approach provides the opportunity for emphasizing the intellectual aspects of a firm's capital. To increase productivity through human capital, the firm needs to harness the potential contribution of the employees and this human capital must then be developed and managed as a core competence of the firm, treating employees as a source of competitive advantage (Barney 1991). Specific HR practices could then be used to enhance the human capital of employees (Youndt et al. 1996), which, in turn, means that the HR practices are indicators of the firm's investment in its HR (Snell and Dean 1992).

Specific examples of HR practices include: selective staffing, training and providing equitable rewards. Together, these practices outline an integrated and strategic approach to HRM that involves designing and implementing a set of internally consistent practices and policies that attempt to harness successfully the firm's human capital, particularly employees' collective knowledge, skills and abilities, towards the achievement of its business objectives (Huselid et al. 1997).

For example, comprehensive training is a standard means of building the skills and competence of employees. The extent to which an organization invests in the development of its employees is a key mechanism for increasing the productivity and, subsequently, the value, of employees (Koch and McGrath 1996).

Studies in the public health sector have found that one way of increasing the level of competency within the public health sector is to tie competencies to reward and performance management (Lichtveld and Cioffi 2003) and the usage of linking reward and compensation systems (Bryson *et al.* 1996). Firms can place more emphasis on selective tests and other human capital-enhancing HR practices as a means of minimizing the mismatch between individuals and the objectives of the firm (Snell and Dean 1992).

Similarly, a direct means of improving or increasing the stock of competence within the firm is through the employees recruited (Parnes 1984). Hiring staff selectively is a method that is increasingly important for companies requiring high-ability employees (Snell and Dean 1992). That is, the more effort the employer is willing to put in to selecting new staff, the better the competence value of employees (Koch and McGrath 1996).

Another HRM element that is part of the repertoire available to managers is the use of equitable reward systems (Snell and Dean 1992). Equitable reward systems aim to provide benefits to the organization from retaining and motivating employees higher than that of the cost savings obtainable from hiring more often from the labour market (Cascio 1991). These practices represent the tactical and strategic components of a strategic approach to HRM that attempts to harness the organization's human capital towards the achievement of its business objectives (Huselid *et al.* 1997). Within the HS sector, HR practices have been adopted to enhance human capital by Canadian nursing homes to deploy their human capital and have been found to have a positive relationship with nursing home performance (Rondeau and Wagar 2001). Subsequently, the combined strategic approach and HR components represent the attempts of the organization to harness their human capital to improve their organization's performance.

Hypothesis 3: Strategic HRM is positively related to perceptions of firm performance in the health services firms (e.g. organizations with higher levels of strategic HRM will have higher levels of performance).

Organizational demographics

Organizational demographics such as size and organizational type (i.e. whether for-profit or non-profit) could play an important role in determining which characteristics can provide the firm with competitive advantage. As Huselid and his colleagues (1997) suggest, HRM effectiveness may not be generalizable to firms competing in environments characterized by lower levels of institutionalization for technical HRM activities. One of these factors is the size of the organization. Size has been often examined in terms of number of employees (Beamish *et al.* 1999) and it has been found to have an influence on the adoption of HRM and the degree and number of HR practices (Hornsby and Kuratko 1990; Duberley and Walley 1995).

Hypothesis 4: Larger HS organizations are more likely to adopt strategic HRM than smaller HS organizations.

Similarly, the size of the organization is often a factor that may impact on its performance, although size is commonly incorporated as a control variable when predicting performance (e.g. Delaney and Huselid 1996).

Hypothesis 5: Larger HS organizations are more likely to perform better than smaller HS organizations.

Testing the direct impact of NPM

Research from the public sector management literatures (e.g. Boyne *et al.* 1999; Rondeau and Wagar 2001) have demonstrated that there are some similarities and differences in HRM adoption, depending on whether the firm originates from the profit or non-profit sector. With the adoption of New Public Management culture in the public sector, commercialized agencies have been found to adopt more strategic HRM than those who have yet to advance in commercialization and corporatization (Teo and Rodwell 2003).

While similarities and differences still exist in the adoption of strategic HRM, Pfeffer (1994) and Youndt and colleagues (1996) argue strongly for the universalistic approach to HRM. These scholars (see discussion by Pfeffer 1994 and Delery and Doty 1996) suggest that as a result of the increasing need to be competitive, firms have to adopt best practice HRM systems that transcend sector. Given the size of the Australian health industry and its competitive and heavily politicized terrain (Braithwaite 1993; Stanton 2000; EOHCS 2001), we would expect HS firms in Australia to adopt the best practice HRM systems. Hence, we hypothesize that:

Hypothesis 6: HS firms in the Australian health service sector will emphasize Commitment to Employees, Customer Demandingness and strategic HRM in the same manner, irrespective of their organizational type (i.e. whether they are for-profit or non-profit).

The underlying model that is the focus of this research project, reflected by the earlier hypotheses, and the model to be tested, is shown in Figure 1.

METHOD

Sample

The sample was drawn from a Dun and Bradstreet list of all of the companies in the selected industry that had greater than fifty employees. Industry effects were controlled for by focusing on a single industry (as per Becker and Gerhart 1996). The respondents were drawn from the Australian health services sector. Upon telephone follow-up, more than 21 per cent of the organizations were excluded from the list due to

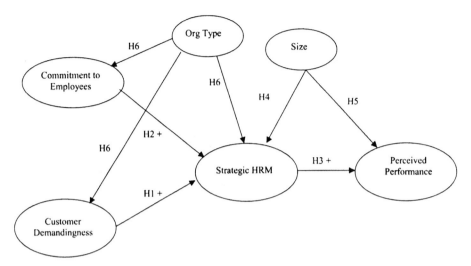

Figure 1: Model of path analysis: Strategic HRM in the Australian health care sector

erroneous information (e.g. number of employees was actually < 50, core Standard Industry Classification (SIC) was incorrect and inappropriate). Altogether 32 per cent of the organizations ($n = 61$) responded to the survey. The sample comprised of 34.4 per cent from the general medical and surgical hospitals (SIC 8,062), followed by 14.8 per cent nursing care hospitals (SIC 8,051) and 16.4 per cent ambulatory surgical centres (SIC 8,011). These organizations employed an average of 557 full-time equivalent employees, ranging from 50 to 7,000 employees.

The survey was typically sent to the Managing Director or General Manager due to their direct knowledge of organizational performance. Almost 54 (53.8) per cent of the respondents were designated as chief executive officer.

Measures

The questionnaire consists of both formative measures (observed indicators that cause or form the latent constructs) and reflective measures (observed indicators that are caused or formed by the latent constructs). The Cronbach alphas for all of the scales were fair to good, ranging from 0.60 to 0.86 and are presented in Table 1.

Organizational orientation (reflective measures)
The scales used for the more contextual strategic and marketing issues were the OCE scale, based on Lee and Miller (1999) and the level of Customer Demandingness faced

by the organization, assessed using the Li and Calantone (1998) Customer Demandingness scale.

Strategic HRM (reflective measures)

Strategic HRM is composed of the degree of strategic HRM in the firm (adopted from Huselid 1995) and all four of the human capital HR scales used by Snell and Dean (1992). Specifically, the human capital measures used were: selective staffing, comprehensive training, performance appraisal and equitable reward systems. Together, these represent a coverage of the domain space of strategic HRM both in terms of explicit practices employed (using the Snell and Dean scales) and the degree to which these practices are present and integrated within a strategic approach to HRM (using the Huselid strategic HRM scale).

Perceived Performance (reflective measures)

Firm performance has been operationalized in the research to include both subjective (Fey and Bjorkman 2001) and financial (Becker et al. 2001) measures. Although perceptual data introduce limitations through increased measurement error and the potential for monomethod bias, it is not unprecedented to use them to measure firm performance (Becker and Huselid 1998) and they have been shown to be strongly correlated with objective measures (Venkatraman and Ramanujam 1987). Further, researchers recommend the use of perceptual performance measures if the sample population contains both profit and non-profit organizations, particularly due to the often inappropriate nature of financial measures for non-profit organizations (Delaney and Huselid 1996; Rondeau and Wagar 2001). Hence, objective measures of firm performance were not used, but indicators of organizational and market performance were used, given that the HS industry has a specific market with comparable, competing firms, and that it would be difficult to find comparable financial performance measures.

Following previous studies (Johansson and Yip 1994; Teo and Rodwell 2003) we set the dependent construct (Perceived Performance) as having a reflective specification. We have operationalized organizational performance by adopting two subjective performance measures from Delaney and Huselid (1996). Respondents were asked to answer questions (1) to evaluate their organization's performance as compared to similar organizations over the past three years (Perceived Organizational Performance, seven items) and (2) to evaluate the performance of the firm over the last three years relative to product market competitors (Perceived Market Performance).

A number of organizational variables that have been found to have an effect on the evaluation of strategic HRM and firm performance were included as control variables. In a similar manner to Rondeau and Wagar (2001), we examined the first check variable, 'Organizational Type', by creating a dichotomous variable differentiating between for-profit and non-profit organization. Organizational size was operationalized by asking the respondents for the total number of full-time equivalent employees. The control variable 'firm size' was obtained by calculating a natural logarithm of the total number of employees (Kimberly 1976).

Model estimation and data analysis
Analyses of all hypotheses were carried out using the Partial Least Square (PLS) latent path model, a well-established technique for estimating path coefficients in causal models (e.g. Johansson and Yip 1994). The conceptual core of PLS is an iterative combination of principal components analysis relating measures to constructs, and path analysis permitting the construction of a system of constructs (Barclay et al. 1995). The PLS technique, compared with LISREL, has several advantages (for a detailed discussion please refer to Johansson and Yip 1994). Among its advantages, PLS can accept smaller sample sizes because 'each causal subsystem sequence of paths is estimated separately. . . . and is particularly suitable for studies in the early stages of theory development and testing' (Anderson and Gerbing 1988, cited in Johansson and Yip 1994: 587). In PLS, the path coefficients are standardized regression coefficients, where the coefficients are similar to factor loadings. The significance of the variables is then determined according to the bootstrap procedure packaged in the PLS-Graph Version 3 software (Chin and Frye 2001).

Validity and reliability issues
The aim of the current study is to further test and develop the constructs of interest for the health services sector context. Subsequently, we followed the recommendation that the covariance-based full-information estimation methods in PLS are considered to be more appropriate for this type of study (Chin 1997).

Harmann's ex post one-factor test was used to provide an additional check for common method variance (Podsakoff and Organ 1986). All of the variables used in the current study were entered into an unrotated factor analysis to determine the number of factors. If a single factor emerged from the factor analysis, that result would indicate that the data suffered from a common method variance problem. In the current study, factor analysis of the variables used in the study resulted in six factors, which provided confidence that common method variance was not an issue.

RESULTS

Descriptive statistics and correlations are reported in Table 1. Most of the human capital-enhancing HR practices are correlated with the performance indicators.

Table 1: Descriptive statistics, correlations and reliabilities of variables

	Mean	SD	1	2	3	4	5	6	7	8	9	10
1 Org size	557	1,171	—									
2 OCE	22.56	2.97	-.07	(0.60)								
3 Customer demandingness	20.88	3.76	-.10	.22	(0.60)							
4 Strategic HRM	26.52	4.02	.018	.46***	.026	(0.81)						
5 Selective staffing	32.31	4.43	-.08	.22	.34*	.35**	(0.73)					
6 Comprehensive training	38.89	7.00	-.13	.33*	.12	.37**	.32*	(0.86)				
7 Equitable reward systems	33.90	5.41	-.17	.16	.13	.13	.22	.29*	(0.66)			
8 Performance appraisal	39.33	5.80	-.10	.24	.30*	.44***	.40**	.47***	.44**	(0.74)		
9 Perceived market performance	11.74	2.15	.06	.16	.03	.27*	.09	.29*	.04	.20	(0.66)	
10 Perceived organisational performance	22.07	3.01	-.05	.40**	.07	.39**	.22	.49***	.23	.32*	.57***	(0.81)

* $p < .05$; ** $p < .01$; *** $p < .001$ correlation is significant at the .05 level (2-tailed), all figures in parentheses on the diagonal are the Cronbach's alpha for each scale, where applicable.

Commitment to Employees is also correlated with strategic HRM and Perceived Performance. The two performance variables are highly correlated with each other.

Figure 2 shows the relationships between the HR and organizational independent variables and Perceived Performance, the dependent variable ($R^2 = 0.418$). As shown in Figure 2, there is a positive and significant path from Customer Demandingness to strategic HRM (coefficient = 0.519, t-statistic = 2.5186, $p < .05$). Hence, Hypothesis 1 was found to be significant, and positive in direction. There was also a positive and statistically significant path from Commitment to Employees to strategic HRM (coefficient = 0.414, t-statistic = 2.5828, $p < .01$), supporting Hypothesis 2. There was a statistically significant path from strategic HRM to Firm Performance and the path was positive (coefficient = 0.645, t-statistic = 3.9558, $p < .001$). Hypothesis 3 was supported. Consistent with the universalistic approach to HRM, we did not find any differences in the link between Customer Demandingness, Commitment to Employees and the adoption of strategic HRM between for profit and non-profit HS firms. Thus Hypothesis 6 was supported. The remaining hypotheses were not supported. Hypotheses 4 and 5 were not supported as there was no size effect on the adoption of strategic HRM and Perceived Performance.

DISCUSSION

The current study applies path analysis modeling to estimate the relationships between Customer Demandingness (external orientation), Commitment to Employees (internal

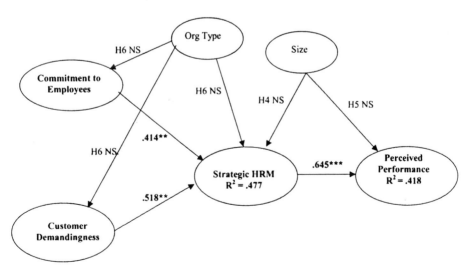

Figure 2: Results of path analysis
NS = not significant; $*p > .05$; $**p > .01$; $***p > .001$;

orientation), strategic HRM and Perceived Performance in the Australian health services sector. The results strongly suggest that in order to enhance the performance of their firms, it is important for their organization to align its external and internal orientation with strategic HRM. The current study provides support for the literature that certain HRM practices can, and do, directly lead to organizational performance in the health sector (e.g. Rondeau and Wagar 2001).

The results did not support the hypothesis that for-profit and non-profit HS firms adopt different levels of strategic HRM. That is, the results support the notion of a best practice approach to strategic HRM (Delery and Doty 1996), irrespective of whether the organization is for-profit or non-profit. The lack of impact of organizational type indicates that HS firms have a large degree of convergence in their strategic HRM systems. In contrast, if organizational type had been significant, then there may have been a case for non-profit organizations to use a public sector specific approach to HRM. Indeed it is possible to argue that this convergence on strategic HRM as a predictor of performance may be either due to industry conditions and/or that the non-profit organizations have adopted NPM to the point where the same factors impact on performance in the same way as for-profit firms.

As highlighted in a number of Australian studies (e.g. Barnett et al. 1996; Stanton et al. 2003), the extent to which the HRM function of the organizations in this study exhibits a strategic orientation is an important differentiator and potential facilitator or source of strategic competencies. Unlike the situation in Hong Kong (Thompson et al. 1999), or the UK (Truss 2003), the Australian health industry seems to have adopted strategic HRM practices as a means of attracting, retaining and maintaining knowledge workers in their organizations, where HRM is often acting as part of a strategic business partnership (Ulrich 1997). Senior executives were able to recognize the importance of acquiring a strategic HRM orientation and the adoption of human capital-enhancing HR practices as the means of enhancing firm performance in the climate of continuous health sector reform in Australia, as in other countries (e.g. Boldy et al. 1996; Thompson et al. 1999).

From a theoretical perspective, the above findings are consistent with the literature on public and non-profit sector management and strategic HRM. First, the above findings highlight the importance of achieving a match between the firm's external orientation (in terms of customer demandingness) and strategic HRM as a means of becoming more marketing and service oriented (Ewing et al. 1999). That is, when organizations have demanding customers placing pressure on them to innovate, they are more likely to have a strategic HRM system in place, or will have built a strategic HRM system to cope with earlier demands from customers.

The link between commitment to employees and strategic HRM highlights the importance of viewing HR as a key source of competitive advantage for knowledge-based firms (Snell et al. 1996; Storey and Quintas 2001), such as those in the sample population. Together the presence of these two orientations lead to strategic HRM, in terms of acquiring a strategic HRM orientation (Huselid 1995) and the adoption of actionable HR practices such as selective staffing, comprehensive training and equity reward systems to attract, retain and motivate human capital (Snell and Dean 1992) in the health sector.

The adoption of selective staffing practices provides support for what Sveiby (1997) terms as 'internal structure' in knowledge management. Together with the current level of emphasis on comprehensive training, our results indicate that there is some evidence that knowledge management practices are in place in these HS firms. These practices are useful for enhancing the skills, experience and knowledge, or human capital (Parnes 1984; Davenport 1999) that is essential in the HS sector (Jacobs and Nilakant 1996; Lichtveld and Cioffi 2003).

The evidence suggests that as the health sector experiences more global reform in terms of policy and managerial changes (EOHCS 2001) Australian HS firms emphasize the buying of skills, experience and knowledge through selective staffing and other human capital-enhancing practices. Researchers such as Snell and Dean (1992) conclude that the adoption of these strategic initiatives are related to the adoption of strategic HRM and those practices that focus on the creation of human capital required for mastering the new managerial and medical systems and techniques. In this instance, HRM has been used to ensure that human resources are selected to add value to the firms' quest for efficiency, effectiveness and economy in the Australian health sector (Barnett et al. 1996; Stanton 2000; Stanton et al. 2003).

Our findings also provide support for the knowledge management literature as HS firms focus on comprehensive training as one of the human capital HR practices necessary to create the core capabilities required for competitive advantage. Given the size of the Australian health industry and its heavily politicized terrain, there was a high degree of knowledge sharing within the industry such that the best practice HRM system was adopted. There is empirical support for the universalistic approach to HRM (Snell and Dean 1992; Pfeffer 1994; Youndt et al. 1996).

This finding has a number of practical implications for HRM in the health services sector. From a practical perspective, the finding implies that the microeconomic and workplace reforms are strongly entrenched within the Australian health industry. The retention of knowledge within HS firms is already in place due to the industry, union and government initiatives put in place to improve the competitiveness of the industry (for example, award restructuring and multi-skilling). Similarly, Jacobs and Nilakant (1996) argue that the adoption of a corporate model of management among public HS firms will facilitate continuous learning and co-ordination across specialist disciplines and team-based organization, achieved through the application of selection techniques, appraisal and reward system that targets team behaviour.

This finding is also supported in the US context by the suggestion of Lichtveld and Cioffi (2003) that one way of increasing the level of competency within the public health sector is to tie competencies to reward and performance management through complementary human resource strategies. Bryson and his colleagues (1996) concur with the usage of linking reward and compensation systems by linking them to performance. It appears that the Australian senior executives in our sample seem to have a similar view, especially in terms of using human capital HR practices to (together with a strategic HRM orientation) enhance firm performance.

The above findings also provide strong support for the changing status of HRM as a profession. The respondents in this study were aware of the continuous push towards the contribution of HRM in strategic management, which is consistent with the empirical findings of senior HR executives in Australia (Fisher et al. 1999). The current findings support the universalistic approach to HRM (Delery and Doty 1996; Youndt et al. 1996) whereby best practice HRM systems have been found to be widespread in the health sector. What lessons could HR practitioners from other countries learn from our current findings? What should HR practitioners do to improve their status and influence within their organizations?

Given the exploratory nature of the current study, the sample size was considered to be sufficient to answer our research questions. There was representation from firms in several Australian states and varied geographical location and size. Despite the small sample size, the individuals who responded were the most senior executives within the HS firms. We relied on the self-typing approach by a single respondent (in this case, the most senior executive) due to the difficulty of gaining a high response rate by matching the responses from multiple respondents. Hence, the results should be interpreted cautiously, given the limitation inherent to this study, that of common method variance as highlighted by Wright and his colleagues (2001). However, this particular methodology is also commonly used by others in international management research (e.g. Leong and Tan 1993) and the results of Harmann's *ex post* one-factor test provided additional support that the problem associating with common method variance is not a major issue in this study.

HR executives could adopt strategies to improve their relationships with senior management. They could put more energy and resources into legitimizing their roles and status within their organizations, especially among the senior management group, the individuals responsible for evaluating the strategic and operational roles (Ulrich 1997; Thompson et al. 1999; Teo and Rodwell 2003). They could strategically explain the benefits of the department's involvement in strategic issues to its multiple constituents. With the progress of reforms rampant in the health sector in Australia and abroad, HR managers could also undertake a proactive role in informing these senior management groups of the need to align the changing values and norms with the changing health landscape. This is similar to what Ulrich (1997) termed as the change agent role. Finally, strategies could be adopted to publicize the success of the HR department in relation to the bottom line of the organizations by becoming strategic business partners to management. If the HRM function is to be strategic in the competitive environment, practitioners should focus on value-adding activities to contribute to the attraction, retention and accessibility of human capital in the health sector. To be effective, practitioners have to move away from administrative roles and position themselves as strategic business partners with multiple stakeholders.

CONCLUSION

The current study has found that the adoption of human capital-enhancing HR practices together with the presence of an external and internal orientation can significantly contribute to firm performance in the health sector. This finding has a number of practical and theoretical implications for HR practitioners in the health sector. By doing so, we have contributed to the health sector employment relations literature, at present, which is considered to be under-developed (see Bach 2000).

Implications for future research

A suggestion for future research is to incorporate into the research design the reliance of multiple stakeholders (Galang 1999) to provide other indicators of strategic HRM effectiveness. Dependent measures such as financial performance indicators could be adopted in order further to minimize common method variance. Future research could examine the development of intellectual capital (not just human capital, but including social and structural capital) across firms and industries to test the model of strategic HRM developed in the current article.

In conclusion, this study contributes towards the literature on the performance of health services firms and their adoption of a strategic approach to HRM across for-profit and non-profit health services firms in the Australian context. Irrespective of whether the organization is for-profit or non-profit, strategic HRM is a key predictor of performance. That is, this study supports the universalistic best practice approach to strategic HRM, and highlights the importance of attracting, retaining and motivating knowledge workers in the health services sector. It is one of the first studies undertaken in a knowledge-intensive context, across for-profit and non-profit organizations in Australia. Our results emphasize the importance of both internal and external issues in achieving strategic HRM, which, in turn, enhances performance in the HS industry. Non-profit organizations in the HS industry need to be aware of both of these orientations in order to adopt strategic HRM – a key consequence, if not requirement, of health sector reform.

REFERENCES

Aulich, C., Halligan, J. and Nutley, S. (2001) *Australian Handbook of Public Sector Management*, South Melbourne: Unwin.

Australian Bureau of Statistics (ABS) (2003) 'Labor Employment by Industry and Occupation' in *Year Book Australia 2003*. Canberra: Australian Bureau of Statistics.

Australia Institute of Health Welfare (AIHW) (2002) 'Australia's Health 2002'. Available at http://www.aihw.gov.au/publications/.

Bach, S. (2000) 'Health Sector Reform and Human Resource Management: Britain in Comparative Perspective'. *International Journal of Human Resource Management*, 11 pp925–42.

Barclay, D., Higgins, C. and Thompson, R. (1995) 'The Partial Least Squares (PLS) Approach to Causal Modeling: Personal Computer Adoption and Use as an Illustration'. *Technology Studies*, 2 pp285–324.

Barnett, S., Buchanan, D., Patrickson, M. and Maddern, J. (1996) 'Negotiating the Evolution of the HR Function: Practical Advice from the Health Care Sector'. *Human Resource Management Journal*, 6:4 pp18–37.

Barney, J. (1991) 'Firm Resources and Sustained Competitive Advantage'. *Journal of Management*, 17 pp99–120.

Barney, J. B. and Wright, P. M. (1998) 'On Becoming a Strategic Partner: The Role of Human Resources in Gaining Competitive Advantage'. *Human Resource Management*, 37 pp31–46.

Beamish, P. W., Karavis, L., Goerzen, A. and Lane, C. (1999) 'The Relationship between Organizational Structure and Export Performance'. *Management International Review*, 39:1 pp37–54.

Becker, B. and Gerhart, B. (1996) 'The Impact of Human Resource Management on Organizational Performance: Progress and Prospects'. *Academy of Management Journal*, 39 pp779–801.

Becker, B. E. and Huselid, M. A. (1998) 'High Performance Work Systems and Firm Performance: A Synthesis of Research and Managerial Implications'. *Research in Personnel and Human Resources Management*, 16 pp53–101.

Becker, B. E., Huselid, M. A. and Ulrich, D. (2001) *The HR Scorecard: Linking People, Strategy, and Performance*, Boston, MA: Harvard Business School.

Becker, G. S. (1993) *Human Capital*, Chicago, IL: University of Chicago Press.

Beer, M., Spector, B., Lawrence, P. R., Mills, D. Q. and Walton, R. E. (1984) *Managing Human Assets*, Boston, MA: Harvard Business School.

Boldy, D., Jain, S. and Chen, G. (1996) 'Comparative Attributes of Effective Health Services Managers and Definitions of Organizational Effectiveness in Australia, the UK and the USA'. *Health Services Management Research*, 9 pp1–9.

Boyne, G., Jenkins, G. and Poole, M. (1999) 'Human Resource Management in the Public and Private Sectors: An Empirical Comparison'. *Public Administration*, 77 pp407–20.

Braithwaite, J. (1993) 'Identifying the Elements in the Australian Health-Service Management Revolution'. *Australian Journal of Public Administration*, 52 pp415–30.

Bryson, C., Jackson, M. and Leopold, J. (1996) 'Human Resource Management in NHS Trusts'. *Health Services Management*, 9 pp98–106.

Cascio, W. F. (1991) *Costing Human Resources*, Boston, MA: PWS-Kent.

Chin, W. W. (1997) 'Overview of the PLS Method'. Available at http://disc-nt.cba.uh.edu/chin/PLSINTRO.HTM.

Chin, W. W. and Frye, T. (2001) *PLS-Graph Software, Version 3*, Houston, TX: University of Houston.

Davenport, T. O. (1999) *Human Capital: What It Is and Why People Invest It*, San Francisco, CA: Jossey-Bass.

Delaney, J. T. and Huselid, M. A. (1996) 'The Impact of Human Resource Management Practices on Perceptions of Organizational Performance'. *Academy of Management Journal*, 39 pp949–69.

Delery, J. E. and Doty, D. H. (1996) 'Modes of Theorizing in Strategic Human Resource Management: Tests of Universalistic, Contingency, and Configurational Performance Predictions'. *Academy of Management Journal*, 39 pp802–35.

Duberley, J. P. and Walley, P. (1995) 'Assessing the Adoption of HRM by Small and Medium-Sized Manufacturing Organizations'. *International Journal of Human Resource Management*, 6 pp891–909.

European Observatory on Health Care Systems (EOHCS) (2001) *Health Care Systems in Transition: Australia*, Copenhagen, Denmark: COHCS.

Ewing, M. T., Ramaseshan, B. and Caruana, A. (1999) 'An Internal Marketing Approach to Public Sector Management: The Marketing and Human Resources Interface'. *International Journal of Public Sector Management*, 12 pp17–26.

Fey, C. F. and Bjorkman, I. (2001) 'The Effect of Human Resource Management Practices on MNC Subsidiary Performance in Russia'. *Journal of International Business Studies*, 32 pp59–75.

Fisher, C., Dowling, P. J. and Garnham, J. (1999) 'The Impact of Changes to the Human Resources Function in Australia'. *International Journal of Human Resource Management*, 10 pp501–14.

Galang, M. C. (1999) 'Stakeholders in High-Performance Work Systems'. *International Journal of Human Resource Management*, 10 pp287–305.

Guthrie, J. P. (2001) 'High Involvement Work Practices, Turnover and Productivity: Evidence from New Zealand'. *Academy of Management Journal*, 44 pp180–90.

Hall, R. (1993) 'A Framework Linking Intangible Resources and Capabilities to Sustainable Competitive Advantage'. *Strategic Management Journal*, 14 pp607–18.

Hornsby, J. S. and Kuratko, D. F. (1990) 'Human Resource Management in Small Business: Critical Issues for the 1990s'. *Journal of Small Business Management*, 29 pp9–18.

Hoskisson, R. E., Hitt, M. A., Wan, W. P. and Yiu, D. (1999) 'Theory and Research in Strategic Management: Swings of a Pendulum'. *Journal of Management*, 25 pp417–56.

Huselid, M. A. (1995) 'The Impact of Human Resource Management Practices on Turnover, Productivity and Corporate Financial Performance'. *Academy of Management Journal*, 38 pp635–72.

Huselid, M. A., Jackson, S. E. and Schuler, R. S. (1997) 'Technical and Strategic Human Resource Management Effectiveness as Determinants of Firm Performance'. *Academy of Management Journal*, 40 pp171–88.

Jacobs, K. and Nilakant, V. (1996) 'The Corporatization of Health Care: An Evaluation and an Alternative'. *Health Services Management Research*, 9 pp107–14.

Johansson, J. K. and Yip, G. S. (1994) 'Exploiting Globalization Potential: US and Japanese Strategies'. *Strategic Management Journal*, 15 pp579–601.

Kimberly, J. (1976) 'Organizational Size and the Structuralist Perspective'. *Administrative Science Quarterly*, 21 pp571–97.

Koch, M. J. and McGrath, R. G. (1996) 'Improving Labor Productivity: Human Resource Management Policies Do Matter'. *Strategic Management Journal*, 17 pp335–54.

Lee, J. and Miller, D. (1999) 'People Matter: Commitment to Employees, Strategy and Performance in Korean Firms'. *Strategic Management Journal*, 20 pp579–93.

Leong, S. M. and Tan, T. T. (1993) 'Managing across Borders: An Empirical Test of the Bartlett and Ghoshal [1989] Organizational Typology'. *Journal of International Business Studies*, 24 pp449–64.

Li, T. and Calantone, R. J. (1998) 'The Impact of Market Knowledge Competence on New Product Advantage: Conceptualization and Empirical Examination'. *Journal of Marketing*, 62 pp13–29.

Lichtveld, M. Y. and Cioffi, J. P. (2003) 'Public Health Workforce Development: Progress, Challenges, and Opportunities'. *Journal of Public Health Management Practice*, 9 pp443–50.

Narine, L. and Persaud, D. D. (2003) 'Gaining and Maintaining Commitment to Large-Scale Change in Healthcare Organizations'. *Health Services Management Research*, 16 pp179–87.

Organization for Economic Co-operation and Development (OECD) (1996) *The Knowledge-Based Economy*, Paris: OECD.

Parker, R. and Bradley, L. (2000) 'Organisational Culture in the Public Sector: Evidence from Six Organisations'. *International Journal of Public Sector Management*, 13 pp125–41.

Parnes, H. S. (1984) *People Power*, Beverly Hills, CA: Sage Publications.

Pfeffer, J. (1994) *Competitive Advantage through People*, Boston, MA: Harvard Business School Press.

Podsakoff, P. and Organ, D. (1986) 'Self Reports in Organizational Research: Problems and Prospects'. *Journal of Management*, 12 pp531–44.

Roberts, J. (2000) 'From Know-How to Show-How? Questioning the Role of Information and Communication Technologies in Knowledge Transfer'. *Technology Analysis and Strategic Management*, 12 pp429 – 43.

Rodwell, J. J. and Teo, S. T. T. (2000) 'Approaches to HRM on the Pacific Rim: A Comparison across Ownership Categories in the Australian Hospitality Industry'. *Research and Practice in Human Resource Management*, 8 pp135 – 51.

Rondeau, K. V. and Wagar, T. H. (2001) 'Impact of Human Resource Management Practices on Nursing Home Performance'. *Health Services Management Research*, 14 pp192 – 202.

Russell, S., Bennett, S. and Mills, A. (1999) 'Reforming the Health Sector: Towards a Healthy New Public Management'. *Journal of Management Development*, 11 pp767 – 75.

Ryan, S. (1993) 'Performance Monitoring and Evaluation: Rationality and Realism'. *Australian Journal of Public Administration*, 52 pp252 – 5.

Schneider, B. (1994) 'HRM – a Service Perspective: Towards a Customer-Focused HRM'. *International Journal of Service Industry Management*, 5:1 pp64 – 76.

Schuler, R. (1992) 'Strategic Human Resource Management: Linking the People with the Strategic Needs of the Business'. *Organizational Dynamics*, 21:1 pp18 – 32.

Schultz, T. W. (1961) 'Investment in Human Capital'. *American Economic Review*, LI:1 pp1 – 16.

Shore, L. M. and Wayne, S. J. (1993) 'Commitment and Employee Behavior'. *Journal of Applied Psychology*, 78 pp774 – 80.

Slater, F. S. and Narver, J. C. (1995) 'Market Orientation and the Learning Organization'. *Journal of Marketing*, 59:July pp63 – 74.

Snell, S. A. and Dean, J. W., Jr (1992) 'Integrated Manufacturing and Human Resource Management: A Human Capital Perspective'. *Academy of Management Journal*, 35 pp467 – 504.

Snell, S. A., Youndt, M. A. and Wright, P. M. (1996) 'Establishing a Framework for Research in Strategic Human Resource Management: Merging Resource Theory and Organizational Learning'. *Research in Personnel and Human Resource Management*, 14 pp61 – 90.

Stanton, P. (2000) 'Employment Relationships in Victorian Public Hospitals: The Kennett Years'. *Australian Health Review*, 23:3 pp193 – 200.

Stanton, P., Bartram, T. and Harbridge, R. (2003) 'Our People Are Our Best Asset: The Promise of HRM in Public Healthcare Facilities'. Conference Proceedings of the Australian and New Zealand Academy of Management Annual Conference, Fremantle, Australia, December.

Storey, J. and Quintas, P. (2001) 'Knowledge Management and HRM' in J. Storey (ed.) *Human Resource Management: A Critical Text* (2nd edn). London: Thomson Learning.

Sveiby, K. E. (1997) *The New Organizational Wealth*, San Francisco, CA: Berrett-Koehler Publishers.

Teece, D. J. (1998) 'Capturing Value from Knowledge Assets: The New Economy, Markets for Know-How and Intangible Assets'. *California Management Review*, 40:3 pp55 – 79.

Teo, S. T. T. and Rodwell, J. J. (2003) 'HR Involvement, Strategic Integration and Performance of Public Sector HR Departments in Australia' in D. H. Nagao (ed.) *Proceedings of the Sixty Third Annual Meetings of the Academy of Management (CD)*, 4 – 7 August. Seattle, USA: The Academy of Management.

Thompson, D., Snape, E. and Stokes, C. (1999) 'Health Services Reform and Human Resource Management in Hong Kong Public Hospitals'. *International Journal of Health Planning and Management*, 14 pp19 – 39.

Truss, C. (2003) 'Strategic HRM: Enablers and Constraints in the NHS'. *International Journal of Public Sector Management*, 16 pp48 – 60.

Ulrich, D. (1992) 'Strategic and Human Resource Planning: Linking Customers and Employees'. *Human Resource Planning*, 15 pp47 – 62.

———— (1997) *Human Resource Champions*, Boston, MA: Harvard Business School.

Venkatraman, N. and Ramanujam, V. (1987) 'Measurement of Business Economic Performance: An Examination of Method Convergence'. *Journal of Management*, 13:1 pp109 – 22.

Vicere, A. A. (2000) 'New Economy, New HR'. *Employment Relations Today*, Autumn pp1 – 11.

Wheelwright, S. C. and Clark, K. B. (1992) *Revolutionizing Product Development*, New York: Free Press.

Wright, P. M., Dunford, B. B. and Snell, S. A. (2001) 'Human Resources and the Resource Based View of the Firm'. *Journal of Management*, 27 pp701 – 21.

Youndt, M. A., Snell, S. A., Dean, J. W., Jr and Lepak, D. P. (1996) 'Human Resource Management, Manufacturing Strategy, and Firm Performance'. *Academy of Management Journal*, 39 pp836 – 66.

Zack, M. H. (1999) 'Developing a Knowledge Strategy'. *California Management Review*, 41:3 pp125 – 45.

FURTHER EDUCATION AND TRAINING IN THE FRENCH PUBLIC SECTOR

A difficult relationship with human resource management

Philippe Méhaut and Coralie Perez

Although the French public sector has made innovations in several fields (e.g. job classifications and hierarchy) and diffused them into the private sector, it has not played the same dynamic role in the field of Further Vocational Education and Training (FVET). Since 1989, the French public sector has imitated the private sector's FVET mechanisms. But today, it seems that just as in the private sector, FVET policies in the public sector have severe limitations. In the private sector, some changes have occurred. Competency-based management has become more important (Klarsfeld and Oiry 2003; Méhaut 2004). Private employers' organizations and unions have recently signed a national collective agreement reforming the institutional framework (Merle 2004). Emphasis is put on employees' career development and mobility, and on broader opportunities of access to FVET in a more long-term perspective.

In the public sector, which represents over 20 per cent of the total labour force (including state administration, hospitals and local administrations), the question of employees' training does not seem to be a priority despite the major challenges this sector will have to face in the years to come.

Demographic evolutions (high level of retirements and decreasing number of young new comers on the labour market) will reinforce pressure on recruitment opportunities and will probably lead to a more active management of the internal labour market.

Moreover, the process of decentralization, as well as changes in certain public departments and the privatization of others (growth of the health service, decrease in the road maintenance) will modify the balance between occupations and between national and local administrations: an increasing need for skilled civil servants is anticipated. The skilling process goes hand in hand with the new demands from the users of public services.

And, although globalization does not exert direct pressure on public services (except for example on public research activities), indirect pressure results from the scarcity of public budget resources.

A more active human resources development (HRD) breaking with the traditional management of the different civil servant corps, has become a necessity. And from this perspective, FVET could be regarded as one of the major tools.

The public sector is not without assets. The life-long tenure system favours investment in human capital, without the threat of poaching policies. Besides, the notion of public service constitutes a motivation for civil servants to adapt so that they can exercise their mission in good conditions. As we will see later, public sector employees are more committed to FVET than private sector employees. But there are many obstacles, including a lack of strategic perspectives from some administrations, weak ties between HRD and FVET, boundaries between the different corps and a possible clash between the notion of FVET as an individual right for the employees and the notion of training as a tool within learning organizations.

This article is based, on the one hand, on a case study of a big public research institute – referred to as 'RESEARCH' here – (9,000 employees). On the other hand, it uses national data originating from a recent survey on access to FVET, which makes it possible to compare the private and public sectors.[1] The survey provides abundant quantitative data on FVET.

The case study, despite the specifics of the research sector, provides a comprehensive analysis of the FVET policy in a public organization.

Section 1 describes the FVET institutional framework in France for the private and public sectors. Section 2 examines the development of FVET structure and policy in RESEARCH and the tension between the notion of FVET as an individual right and the notion that it is a tool for the organization. Section 3 compares some

---

The data are drawn from the 'Continuing Training 2000' survey which complements the Employment survey conducted by the French National Statistics Institute (INSEE) in March 2000. 'Continuing Training 2000' was mainly designed by Céreq and INSEE.

The survey was carried out on a sample of 28,700 individuals who were under 65 years of age, had completed their formal training and were not doing their military service at the time. These individuals were asked questions, in face-to-face interviews, concerning their training experiences after leaving the educational system, and more detailed questions were asked concerning the fourteen months prior to the survey. The survey takes into account training activities, regardless of the goal (explicitly professional or more personal). But, in order to be identified as a training activity, the act must be intentional, it must have lasted at least three hours and be organized in some way. It encompasses several forms of training: adult educational and training programmes, classroom instruction, lectures, tutorials, seminars, on-the-job training, self-training (including distance learning) and alternating training (apprenticeship for adults in the framework of public employment policies). The survey provides detailed information about the training undergone by individuals in the previous fourteen months (on whose initiative was the course?, does training infringe on leisure time?, and so on). Moreover, one original feature of the survey is that both training courses participants and non-participants were interviewed about their job environment and were asked how much they knew about the different training opportunities available to them. The number of people employed in France's public service was estimated from INSEE's Employment survey, on the basis of the legal status and activity of the institutions employing the individuals interviewed. In all, the number of public-service employees was estimated at 5,260,000. Between January 1999 and February 2000, over 2,400,000 of these employees participated to a total of 4,350,000 training activities of more than 3 hours each.

Figure 1: The 'Continuing Training 2000' survey

> The data and information used in this case study analysis comes from the work of an evaluating committee of the FVET policy. For six months, this tripartite committee (RESEARCH managers, RESEARCH union representatives and external experts, including one of the authors who chaired the committee) examined the main components of the FVET policy. The tripartite committee gathered a lot of quantitative and qualitative data provided by the training department and by external experts (including some special reports and statistics especially developed for the committee): rate of access to the courses, fields of training, management of the training policy... He also interviewed managers, training officers. The report was delivered at the end of 2003 to the RESEARCH top management, so as to encourage them to develop a new FVET policy. The analysis of the data and information presented in this article is the sole responsibility of the authors.

Figure 2: RESEARCH case study: data and methodology

quantitative indicators of the FVET policy of RESEARCH with the public sector as a whole and private organizations, and enables us to identify some characteristics that are specific to the public sector. The concluding section, based on our analyses, paves the way for a debate on key issues for a closer link between FVET and the HRD approaches.

FVET IN THE FRENCH PUBLIC SECTOR: A REPRODUCTION OF THE PRIVATE SECTOR'S MECHANISM BUT IN A DIFFERENT CONTEXT

FVET within organizations is more institutionalized in France than in other European countries.

When the public sector lost its leadership

During the thirty years following World War II, the French public sector[2] strongly influenced the private sector in terms of employment regulations: seniority rules, national system of classification (the system of classification built up after World War II for the private sector was partly inspired by the public job classification and hierarchy), health and safety regulations. Unions often used to take the example of the public sector in their discussion with private employers.

Surprisingly, with regards to FVET regulation, it was the private sector that influenced the public sector. The FVET system in the private sector, which has no equivalent in Europe, was based upon a multi-sector agreement signed in 1970, the principles of which were reiterated in the legislation passed in 1971.

The system is based, first of all, on the company's obligation to allocate a percentage of the total wage bill to employee training: 0.8 and later 0.9 per cent of the company's total wage bill must be invested in an employee training scheme chosen and implemented by the employer; 0.1 to 0.7 per cent must be allocated to various compulsory training schemes through compulsory contributions to government or group funds (e.g. personal training leave, alternance training for young people). Second, it is based on an employee-training plan, implemented by the company and discussed with the work council (whose opinion is not binding). The plan must provide for training operations for the year to come; the training must take place during working hours in accordance with the regulation requiring employers to provide adaptation training for their employees. Funds can be pooled (an option mainly used by small and medium enterprises); in this case the firms belonging to the fund pay all or part of their contributions into a joint fund, which is then used to reimburse the company for its training expenses or to organize its own group training schemes.

Last, beside the above-mentioned measures, which are essentially implemented at the employer's initiative, an employee may take personal training leave at his or her own initiative.

These two paths (training plan within the firm and individual training leave) reflected the tension between two conceptions of FVET, which was seen, on the one hand, as an organizational tool chosen and controlled by the employer and, on the other, as an individual right disconnected from the employment relationship. The notion of training as an organizational tool now tends to prevail in the private sector and individual training leaves are seldom taken (Mehaut 1995). But the conception of further education as an individual right was strongly supported by some unions and a good number of teachers and trainers.

Even if the public sector was formally included in the 1971 law, it later adopted the private sector's framework, reproducing the same tension between the two paths. Indeed, in 1983, a law defined further education and training as a right and an obligation for civil servants. On the one hand an individual training leave was created, based on the private sector's system, but with larger facilities for civil servants. On the other hand, the law emphasized the necessity for civil servants to adapt to an ever-changing environment. The 'activation' of FVET policies in the public sector was triggered in 1989, in the context of modernization of public services; FVET has since then been considered as a tool for modernization. The aim of this modernization was to bring the State closer to citizens and to make civil servants more accountable to taxpayers. In order to achieve this goal, the temptation to imitate the private sector in several domains, including FVET, was quite strong (Lenoir 1996). A first agreement was signed at national level with trade unions. Two other agreements followed in 1992 and 1996 (Lenoir 1996). They defined quantitative targets (x per cent of the wage bill for FVET, using the average percentage in the private sector as a reference) and more qualitative targets (e.g. higher opportunities of access for the less skilled civil servants, gender equality). In the hospital and local authority sectors, collective funds were set up and contributions were made compulsory.

So the system of further education adopted by public institutions was directly inspired by those of the private sector.

Specificities of the public sector

Despite similarities between the private and public sectors' FVET systems, there are also differences resulting essentially from characteristics that are specific to public institutions.

- The public sector's activities (the importance of public education, public research institutions and of the health systems) require a highly skilled structure: for example, 30 per cent of civil servants have at least a 3-year university degree (against 8 per cent in the private sector); 34 per cent of the employees in public hospitals have a 2-year university degree (against 12 per cent in the private sector). Access to FVET is known to be positively correlated with the level of formal education. A higher probability of access in the public sector and of a more proactive demand from civil servants is therefore probable.
- Recruitment and upward mobility are mainly determined by competitive examinations (for civil servants who represent three-quarters of the employees in the public sector). For most job categories in the civil service, a person cannot be recruited unless he or she has a specific level of education. In order to be promoted to a higher category, one must either pass an examination or be promoted by a national commission, which usually takes into account seniority, performance and competency-development. In both cases, career promotion opportunities depend on job vacancies, which themselves depend on the number of posts (per category) provided for in the annual budget. Individuals have the right to take time to prepare for the examination (special leave, training, etc.). Thus, part of the education and training activity consists in preparing for examinations, on a compulsory basis. Nevertheless, these activities are far from being the major part of FVET courses: they only represented 17 per cent of training courses in 1999 (DGAFP 2001). Thus, because of the weight of seniority on upward mobility and of the very complex distribution of job opportunities between corps (low possibilities of mobility from teaching to research work for example, or between one administration department and another) FVET cannot be viewed as an *active* tool for career development. FVET has more to do with job adaptation, geographical and occupational mobility (which is higher in the

public sector than in the private sector). This tends to reinforce the narrow-minded and short-term oriented conception of FVET (Cieutat 2000).

- In the private sector, the work council must, at least once a year, give recommendations concerning the firm's training plan. Usually a special FVET commission meets once or twice the year in order to study and evaluate the proposals made by the firms. But the work council's recommendations are not binding for the employer. In the public sector, where the rate of unionization is higher, and where a tradition of consensus prevails, similar commissions are set up at various levels. A kind of co-management with the unions has been developed in most public organizations.

These specific characteristics concern all public organizations and impact on the level and nature of FVET efforts and on training practices.

FVET IN A PUBLIC RESEARCH ORGANIZATION: ADMINISTRATIVE RULES, CO-MANAGEMENT AND INDIVIDUAL DEMANDS

We shall now examine the consequences of this situation, for RESEARCH and for the public sector as a whole, and we shall make a few comparisons with the private sector.

RESEARCH: A big public organization

RESEARCH is one of the biggest public research organizations in France; it specializes in agricultural and natural sciences. It comprises over 9,000 people, among whom 1,850 are researchers, 6,600 are engineers, technicians or administrative workers. Over 6,000 employees work in research units. One thousand of them work in specific experimental laboratories and 1,500 in service units (e.g. administration, computer units). Approximately 650 people are PhD students or Post Doctoral graduates, most of them with scholarships. With 46 per cent of the employees belonging to the 'A' category (high-skilled jobs, usually requiring a minimum of a three-year university degree), RESEARCH employs people with slightly higher qualifications than other state administrations do (40%). Its activity is not only pure academic research. It is also involved in applied research and expertise. Due to the organization's experimental activity in agricultural science, part of its low-skilled staff carries out traditional farm work.

The institute is managed by a council, comprising representatives of the industrial sector, trade unions and various French administrations. But it is under strong supervision by the Research and Agriculture ministries that provide 80 per cent of its budget.

The organization is divided into twenty-one plants (laboratories, experimental farms) located across the country, each of them with a local administration, including training officers.

In 1984 the institute's employees obtained the civil servant status. On average, 300 new employees are recruited each year through competitive examinations. Employees have life-long tenure and the labour turnover is very low. A total of 70 per cent of the employees have over 10-year seniority and 15 per cent have over 30-year seniority. Internal mobility is governed by classical civil servant statutory rules. Wages increase essentially according to seniority within a job category. Upward mobility is governed by the same rules as in the public sector. There are rigid boundaries between the researcher category (most researchers are recruited externally) and the other categories. In the last four years, technicians, engineers and administrative workers have had, on average, 250 opportunities of promotion within their category, and 210 opportunities to move from their category to another (of which approximately half through competitive exams) each year.

Employees are represented by three trade unions and more than 70 per cent of the employees vote for representatives.

FVET management: Between co-management and individuals' expectations

As in the public sector, unions and employers 'co-manage' FVET through a joint agreement on the main lines of a FVET plan; the agreement is renewed every three years and is inspired by the national agreements.[3] This joint agreement defines the quantitative target (3.8 per cent of the wage bill for 1998 agreement), as well as other priorities in terms of goals. Bipartite commissions examine the yearly training plans: a national commission, local commissions in each local laboratory and special sub-commissions for some parts of the training plan. The training managers usually follow 'to the letter' the guidelines proposed by the commissions.

By closely examining the two agreements signed at RESEARCH, one can identify two stages in the development of a FVET policy. The first agreement was very much based on the notion of training as an individual social right. It emphasized social promotion – for low-skilled employees essentially – on the one hand, and opportunity for individual choice on the other, even when that choice does not correspond to the individual's job. The committee of evaluation of this first agreement concluded that 'the agreement still fails to propose a global policy that is coherent with and related to the scientific activity of the institute'. It recommended that 'the training needs should be better analysed, and emphasis should be put on the functioning of the work unit rather than on the individual'. Between 1993 and 1998, FVET for researchers was not much developed.

The second agreement takes these elements partly into account. More attention is given to the training of scientists. One section of the agreement specifically deals with the development of a more collective FVET policy at the level of services and research units. But these suggestions have not been put into practice. The agreement is too general and could have been applied to any other administration or organization. The links with the scientific goals of the institute were not explicit. Moreover, the evaluating committee for the second agreement, while acknowledging an improvement, came to similar conclusions as drawn for the first agreement. The general strategic plan of the institute (adopted in 2000) outlines strong and clear scientific orientations and gives strong recommendations for the development of an active human resource management but it says little about the role of FVET. The links are still weak between the strategies of the institute, the human resource policy and the FVET policy. Based on those agreements, the training is managed by a national training department and by local training officers in the local plants. At national level, training managers draw the yearly training plan, manage the budget, generate the training policy, develop national transversal courses and produce data. At local level training officers do the same for the laboratories. They have direct relations with the employees, find out what their needs are (often through a questionnaire) and then draw the yearly training plan for the laboratories. They manage the relationship with training providers and evaluate the quality of the training. From the beginning, in RESEARCH, as in many other organizations, the training department was developed as a separate entity and was not part of the human resources department (which was more a service of administrative management; the HRD department was created in 2001). Nowadays, the process of integration of the training department into the HRD department has only just been completed at local level. But in most laboratories, the training officers continue to gather individuals' needs, and the relation with the work units and their strategic goals is still rather weak. This type of organization is very similar to that of other public services and has produced very similar results in the development of the FVET policy.

INTENSITY AND EQUALITY OF ACCESS AND CONTENTS OF THE FVET POLICY

What are the main lines of FVET policies in RESEARCH and what are the similarities and differences with the public sector as a whole and the private sector?

A higher participation to FVET in RESARCH and in the public sector

Between 1992 and 2002, RESEARCH's FVET expenditures increased, as planned in the two agreements. From 1992 to 1998, the percentage of the wage bill spent on FVET (costs including trainees' wages, direct and indirect training costs) was, on average, 2.5 per cent. From 1998, the spending increased to 3.7 per cent and has been stable since 2001. About 57 per cent of the employees attend training courses each year for an average duration of 38 hours per trainee.[4] This figure is approximately the same as that of the public sector as a whole (3.5 per cent of the wage bill in 2000) and is higher than that of other public research institutes.

A more qualitative approach could give higher results, whether in terms of access rate or in terms of expenditures. Indeed, in the calculation of training expenditures, the formal courses, rather than other modes of training, are taken into account. Unions spend their time discussing the boundaries of FVET and do not consider that participating in a scientific congress, for example, is part of FVET. Part of the more informal training activities (including permanent tacit on-the-job training of the researchers) are not accounted for.

When comparing the public and private sectors (basing ourselves on similar data collected directly from individuals, which also include less formal training such as self-training or participation to conferences, seminars, etc.), the public sector still appears to be more generous than the private sector. The probability of gaining access to training is higher in the public (47%) than in the private sector (33%); furthermore, the average duration of training is higher in the former. Even when the different job positions are taken into account, the results are always higher in the public sector. Individuals in research and applied studies positions have a rate of access to FVET ranging from 57 per cent in the private sector to 61 per cent in the public sector; similar figures are obtained for teachers, as well as for other job positions. This result is confirmed by a logit analysis enabling us to compare individuals with similar characteristics in the public and private sectors (e.g. age, gender, diploma) (Perez 2003). In any case, the opportunity of gaining access to training is higher in the public sector.

A look at the various types of training (see Table 1) shows that, in the public sector, the use of formal classroom training is higher than in the private sector. On-the-job training is not given as much importance.

Three main reasons can be given to explain this higher participation to FVET in RESEARCH and in the public sector as a whole.

First, and in accordance with some hypotheses of the human capital theory, we must consider the impact of the life-long tenure system. On the one hand, the risk of

Table 1: Various training practices

	Public sector (share of trainees)	Private sector (share of trainees)
Formal training (among which	79	70
seminars, conferences)	12	8
On-the-job training	16	26
Self-training	5	4
Total	100	100

Source: Céreq/INSEE, CT2000 survey.

poaching and wasting the training investment is considered lower in the public than in the private sector. This is a good incentive for public employers to develop active training policies. Moreover, as the wage level is ruled by collective regulations and mainly unrelated to performance, the rate of return to training funded by employers could easily be higher. On the other hand, the higher job stability for public employees could enhance their demands for job adaptation and job evolution training. Second, the unions in the public sector are more powerful and FVET is a consensual issue[5]. For the sake of consensus, the management is prepared to meet unions' demands concerning FVET, even if this implies that they be more generous. The wish to reach a consensus could also explain the more equal distribution of FVET (see later). Indeed, the management sometimes uses FVET as a tool to promote modernization and to facilitate broad changes affecting the nature of the work or the civil servant status (as, for instance, the opening of European market for Customs department employees). As a result of this, there is a risk that the FVET issue might be used by management to keep unions 'happy' rather than to improve human resources management. Third, employees in the public sector have a better knowledge of their rights and opportunities than in the private sector (Perez 2003). This could also be due to the fact the management and training departments, and the unions inform the employees better.

A more equal access to FVET than in the private sector

Most studies show that access to FVET varies significantly according to the levels of formal education or to the occupations.

Comparing RESEARCH with the whole public sector, the rate of access per job category shows a more equal distribution in RESEARCH (see Table 2). The opportunity to attend FVET is 53 per cent for the lowest category, 61 per cent for engineers and 48 per cent for researchers. FVET opportunities for researchers increased from 30 per cent in 1996 to 48 per cent in 2000, but not to the detriment of the former. However researchers remain less concerned with formal FVET. This was one of the weaknesses of the first agreement. The second agreement proposed new specific training initiatives, which have successfully been implemented. But researchers probably see their training as being part of their day-to-day activities.

In comparison with the public sector, the private sector shows a higher level of inequality. The rates of access to training are always higher in the public sector than in the private sector whatever the levels of formal education or the occupations; furthermore, the access rate dispersion within a category is always lower. The likelihood of participation to training is higher for a clerical worker in the public sector than for private sector employees with middle-level occupations, once controlled for some basic variables with a logit model. Considering employment status, temporary workers are less disadvantaged in the public sector; 'all things being equal', the fact

Table 2: Access to the FVET[a] according to the job categories (RESEARCH and the public sector) (in %)

Job category[b]	RESEARCH, rate of access to FVET	Public sector – rate of access to FVET	Private sector – rate of access to FEVT
A (engineers and researchers) managers	55	57	53
B (other skilled) Middle-level occupations	62	54	46
C/D (semi or unskilled) Office workers and operatives	53	39	25
Total	56	47	32

Source: Céreq/INSEE, CT2000 survey; evaluation report of the RESEARCH FVET policy.
[a]The rate of access is the percentages of individuals involved in at least one training activity of at least three hours between January 1999 and February 2000.
[b]In the public sector, the job category distinguishes between three levels A, B and C (first rows), which are roughly equivalent to the distinction in the private sector (second rows).

that an employee does not have the civil servant status does not decrease his or her probability of gaining access to FVET (Perez 2003).

Despite a lower inequality of opportunities in the public sector, the classical variables (occupation, level of education, gender) play a similar role in both sectors (Perez 2002). In other words, the disparities are lower in the public sector but of a similar nature: the individuals who are most likely to receive training are those under the age of 50, with higher education levels, in managerial rather than clerical positions. This lower rate of inequality reflects the strong tradition of equality in the public sector, which is embodied in the use of the competitive examinations. But this tradition of equality is probably also due to the role of unions. In RESEARCH, for example, the rights of the lowest categories are an important question for unions. As in the national agreements, the RESEARCH joint agreements set up a kind of affirmative action system for unskilled or semi-skilled employees, and measures are taken to ensure that this system is implemented in practice.

A higher rate of participation to training by civil servants

In RESEARCH, procedures to gather training needs data were introduced with the first agreement. The yearly training plan is mostly based on the gathering of data on employees' needs. In this process, they usually show a high level of individual demand. On the contrary, collective training operations, linked with change in services and/or led by the hierarchy are less developed. The national statistical survey shows how people enter a training course. In terms of courses funded by employers and corresponding to the professional activity, the survey shows that in the private sector, approximately 50 per cent of the trainees declared that they were sent by their employers; 19 per cent declared that they attended the course of their own initiative; and 24 per cent declared it was a joint initiative. In the public sector, the figures are different: 33 per cent were sent to training by their employers; 36 per cent attended a course of their own initiative; and 27 per cent attended a training course as a result of a joint initiative (Fournier *et al.* 2002). This could indicate that in the public sector employees are more proactive in terms of training (and this is probably related to the higher level of education and the fact that employees are better informed about their rights), but also a lower level of commitment from the management.

Short-term courses designed for adaptation

Looking at the nature of the FVET policy, two main dimensions could be analysed.

The duration and the explicit aims of the courses

As pointed out before, in RESEARCH, most courses are short term. Only 17 per cent of the training courses last longer than 100 hours. Similar figures apply for the rest of the public sector and the private sector. In both sectors, short-term courses are the majority (50 per cent < 16 hours in the public and private sectors).

Most courses in RESEARCH could be defined as refresher courses. The CT2000 survey shows a similar picture at national level: 74 per cent of the trainees employed in the public sector declared that the course was aimed at job adaptation (76 per cent in the private sector). Fifteen per cent of the employees in the public sector and 14% of employees in the private sector attend courses in the hope of obtaining a degree and/or of making a career change.

Although RESEARCH's FVET policy is centred essentially on job adaptation, some specific tools were developed in both agreements in order to facilitate access to long-term courses, often leading to a degree (for promotion or occupational conversion) or to develop career guidance. Between 1999 and 2002, 14 per cent of the training hours on average were part of long-term courses, but few employees (no more than 100) attended long-term training. This is probably related to the difficulties in developing an efficient mode of human resource management. The forecasting of future job and skill requirements in the long term is only being conducted now. And the public rules of internal mobility hardly take into account FVET.

The fields of training

In the case of RESEARCH training courses include the following categories: basic scientific domains and technical disciplines (24%), computer science and personal computer use (18%), foreign languages (12%), management and human resources, communication (12%), personal development (8%), health, prevention and safety (8%).

These figures cannot be compared to those of the rest of the public sector, due to problems of categorization and to the specificity of the activity. The contents of the training related to the 'heart of the professional activity' are necessarily different and incomparable. But for other more transversal disciplines, there are many similarities: computer sciences account for about 20 per cent in the public and private sectors, management and communication for 11 per cent, health and security for 8 per cent. As for foreign languages there are significant differences between RESEARCH and the public or private sectors (only 2 per cent in the public sector, 3 per cent in the private sector). Courses in foreign languages are logically less required in the public sector as a whole than in the private sector. But, in the case of RESEARCH, the opposite is true. This reflects the more and more European and worldwide dimension of the research activity.

CONCLUSION: KEY POINTS FOR LINKING FVET, STRATEGY AND HRD

Literature emphasizes more and more the need for a more pro-active or strategic HRD. In the private sector, this need is frequently linked to globalization, market pressure, the development of a knowledge economy (David and Foray 2003). Human resources development is viewed as a key condition of competitiveness (d'Iribarne 1990). Issues such as the learning organization and/or life-long learning are underlined (Amadieu and Cadin 1996; Marsick and Watkins 1999). And the question of a more active use of FVET, as one of the tools of the individual's professional development and of the organization's improvement is on the agenda.

Most analyses show that the private sector still remains far away from that goal. In the French public sector, the weakness of HRD practices is well known even though there have been improvements in the last ten years. In 1998, the French Public Services Ministry asked for an assessment of HRD in the public sector. The subsequent report stated two main problems. The first was the lack of strategy and professionalism of the HRD function. Efforts to develop and transfer good practices between administrations were insufficient, and the role of HRD management was often badly defined and not enough recognized within public organizations. The second problem was that the civil servant status was unfairly mentioned as a barrier to greater HRD development; moreover, 'The status of civil servants and the joint management with unions are sometimes used as an alibi to avoid making innovations even though these innovations are compatible with the civil servant status and the co-management (Vallemont 1999: 115).

Similar conclusions could be drawn about RESEARCH. FVET policy, HRD policy and the strategy of the organization are weakly related. FVET remains mainly based on individuals' demands – more so than in the private sector. And, as in the private sector, FVET mainly consists in short-term job adaptation courses. These conclusions are in keeping with those of a national evaluating committee of FVET in the public sector (Cuby 2003), which were similar to those drawn in the previous 1998 report about HRD. First, the committee emphasizes the drift towards a short-term – on-the-job adaptation – FVET policy, far from a strategic human resource development. Second, it emphasizes the need for a more pro-active involvement of the management, and of a more strategic integration of FVET, both in terms of strategic goals of public services and of human resource management.

In both reports the civil servant status is not considered as an obstacle in itself: the modes of application introduce some rigidities, but its basic rules are quite flexible. The public sector also has more positive figures: a wider and more equal participation to FVET than in the private sector, a higher commitment of individuals. Bearing in mind the challenges for the public sector detailed in the introduction of this article, what are the key questions that must be addressed in order to renew FVET management?

Developing a closer relation between strategy, HRM and FVET

The rather weak relation between FVET and the organization's strategy in RESEARCH could be explained by different factors, which could also be valid for other public organizations.

On the one hand, in RESEARCH as well as in most public organizations (but also in many private firms) the strategic goals of the organization (when they are explicit) are divided between HRD and FVET goals and tools. In RESEARCH, the HRD manager is not a member of the top executive committee. And, as we have seen, the FVET department is rather independent. If the organization's management team does not consider HRD and FVET as key questions for the organization and does not deliver a clear and strong message, the FVET department alone will not be able to promote strategic orientations.

On the other hand, other indicators also show a low level of commitment of the middle management. This low level of commitment is obvious in RESEARCH. The managers of the scientific units, who are themselves scientists, dedicate more of their time to the general management of their units than to human resource management and they do not focus much on FVET issues. As a matter of fact, the yearly evaluation of employees, which addresses training matters, sometimes led to no definite or operational conclusions. Furthermore, the joint agreement procedure also had an indirect consequence on their level of commitment: part of the middle management team was under the impression that FVET was a matter for the top management and the unions, as a component of internal industrial relations and that they should not interfere. More generally, the higher level of individual demands in the public sector (as seen in section 3 'Intensity and equality of access and contents of the FVET policy') could also be considered as an indicator that the management teams in the public sector are less committed than management teams in the private sector. A higher commitment of the management teams is probably a necessary but not sufficient condition for a more pro-active FVET policy.

A renewed balance between individual choices and organization needs

For the unions and employees in the public sector, FVET is mainly seen as a personal (social) right, independent from the organization. This is partly due to the specificity of the relationship with the employer. Indeed, civil servants usually feel that they belong to and depend on the public administration rather than on the specific department in which they work. And the managers of public organizations have little power over their employees' careers. This is also due to trade unions' policies: in the 1980s and 1990s, some unions demanded that employees be granted an absolute right to FVET, independent from the employer's choices. In RESARCH, the second agreement considered FVET as 'a right which must contribute to employees' career development as part of the collective evolution of their work units. The individual project must be more integrated into a collective dynamic, in order to be more successful'. In other words, the individuals' expectations and choices took precedence over the organization. As highlighted before, this does not mean that the employees accord more importance to their extra professional projects than to their professional ones. In terms of training courses, we stated that individuals clearly expressed a 'choice' in favour of job adaptation and refresher courses.[6]

Reinvested in a broader organizational context (organizational change, teamwork) and in a more long-term perspective (individual career development), this strong individual commitment to FVET could have more significance for employees and simultaneously act as a lever for the development of a learning organization.

A wider conception of FVET

In earlier stages of the development of the French FVET system (in the private and public sectors), strong emphasis was put on formal education and training. This was partly due to the conception of formal (general and vocational) education, to the role of diplomas in the classification system (in the private sector) or in the competitive examinations (in the public sector): the only way of acquiring knowledge was thought to be through school, and without school-based education one could not obtain a degree. Just as in other countries, in a changing work organization, the importance of experience and work-based learning is increasingly acknowledged. In a recent national collective agreement, private actors have put the emphasis on a new, broader, conception of the professional development of employees, including various ways of learning, assessment of prior experience (Méhaut 2003). A new law promotes opportunities to obtain degrees (partly or the totality) by recognizing the importance of experience and knowledge acquired at work (Labruyère 2003). As mentioned earlier, a narrow-minded conception of FVET still prevails in the public sector. This is true with regard to the recruitment of individuals as well as to the rest of their careers in the public sector. The experience gained through previous jobs is not recognized, which means that experience is not considered as a substitute for diplomas or for the formal training programmes that all new recruits must attend after passing their competitive entry examination. Broadening this conception of FVET, developing prior learning assessment, on the one hand, and diversifying the ways of acquiring knowledge, on the other could lower the cost of FVET (or increase the level of FVET), and would facilitate recruitment and promote the career evolution of the employees.

The relation between FVET and HRD policy

But the last and probably the most determinant factor is the HRD policy itself and its relation with the FVET policy.

Generally speaking, as shown earlier, the lack of a pro-active human resource management is still a characteristic of RESEARCH and of the public sector (see Cuby 2003 for the public sector as a whole). The human resources department of RESEARCH was only set up in 2001. And the shift to a new style of management is not yet completed.

More specifically, three types of relation between FVET and, first the nature of the job (or job change), second the wage level and third the job position (job mobility and upgrading) must be taken into account.

The relation between FVET and the job (in the short term), is the most usual. As pointed out before, in the public and private sectors, most courses are job adaptation training courses (76 per cent in the private sector, 74 per cent in the public sector). Short-term courses prevail and their duration has decreased. But the nature of the jobs is changing more deeply. And sometimes refresher courses are not enough to adapt to evolutions. A better analysis of these changes is needed. RESEARCH, as well as other public organizations, have recently developed job analysis and forecasting. The need for a closer relation to FVET is recognized but it has not yet been met in practice. This kind of analysis is not contradictory with the civil servant status. But it will generate a shift from a conception based on employment tenure and career (the civil servant is potentially regarded as able to perform any kind of job) to a conception that is much more based on the occupational contents of the job.

The second relation, that between FVET and the wage level could have some meaning in the new competency-based management where competencies are evaluated and included in the wage profile of the individual. But it is still rare in the private sector and even more rare in the public sector. Besides, the CT2000 survey, shows that among the participants in training programmes only 9 per cent of public employees hoped that their participation to a training course would lead to a wage increase (against 14 per cent in the private sector) (no figure available for RESEARCH). Wage increases are higher for employees who participate in training courses than for employees who do not ; but regardless of the sector, these gains are not statistically significant (Goux and Zamora 2001).[7] In the public sector and in RESEARCH, seniority rules prevail, and individuals' efforts in terms of training are seldom or not taken into account. And qualitative analyses of the situation in RESEARCH shows that most employees who had attended a training course felt that the training had no impact upon their incomes. If refresher courses and regular (short-term) job adaptation courses are considered as normal activities for any type of employees, introducing wage incentives for the (long-term) competency development of employees could increase the demand for broader, long-term oriented training solutions. But, although this type of measure is not in itself contradictory with the civil servant status, it might call into question the traditional use of this status. In most cases, wage increase and other premiums are traditionally distributed on an equal basis and do not differ between individuals (with the same seniority level and the same job position).

The third relation, that between FVET and changes in job position and/or promotion, also seems very blurred. In the private sector, various studies have shown that the relation has become weaker. In the public sector, the CT2000 survey shows that there is no relationship between FVET and the changing of category: the rate of access to training is similar for those who are promoted and those who are not (Lowezanin and Perez 2002).[8] In RESEARCH, the mobility is also rather low. And training does not play a significant role. Unfortunately no evaluation of the long-term impact of the specific mechanism dedicated to long-term and qualifying training is available. The general impression of the employees is that training has a very low effect on mobility. This reinforces the prevalence of short-term training courses. However, in the next ten years, demographic constraints will force the different actors concerned to adopt more active mobility policies (within as between public organizations). They will probably be one of the major factors of evolution of the notions of FVET.

NOTES

1   C. Perez was one of the producers of the survey; P. Méhaut was committed by the research institute as the president of the evaluating committee of the FVET policy.

2   Which used to include a number of nationalized firms.

3   The first agreement was concluded in 1993 and the second, concluded in 1998, was extended to 2003.

4   Nineteen hours per course, a trainee attending two courses a year on average.

5   In RESEARCH, where industrial relations are difficult, the bipartite training commissions work there permanently.

6   The RESEARCH second agreement proposed a mechanism specifically designed for individuals' extra professional needs (for individuals' social or political activities, outside the workplace). The level of demand for such training activities was very low.

7   It should be added that before entering into training programmes, wages are higher for participants than
     for non-participants, once controlled for seniority and firm size (about + 10 per cent for clerical and
     operatives and + 5 per cent for managers) (Goux and Zamora 2001).
8   But the sample is small and, more importantly, the duration of observation is rather short (three years).
     Due to the role of examinations, the training courses could have some effects later.

REFERENCES

Amadieu, J. F. and Cadin, L. (1996) *Compétence et Organisation Qualifiante*, Paris: Economica.

Cieutat, B. (2000) *Fonctions Publiques: Enjeux et Stratégies pour le Renouvellement*, Paris: La Documentation Française.

Cuby, J. F. (2003) *La Politique de Formation Continue des Agents de l'État et des Hôpitaux*, Paris: La Documentation Française.

David, P. A. and Foray, D. (2003) 'Economic Fundamentals of the Knowledge Society'. Policy Futures in Education, January.

DGAFP (2001) 'La Formation des Agents de l'Etat en 1999'. Enquête Statistique sur les Actions de Formation Réalisées par les Ministères en Faveur des Agents de l'Etat, April.

D'Iribarne, A. (1990) *La Compétitivité, Défi Social et Éducatif*, Paris: Presses du CNRS.

Fournier, C., Lambert, M. and Perez, C. (2002) 'Les Français et la Formation Continue, Statistiques sur la Diversité des Pratiques'. Marseille: Céreq, no. 169, Série Observatoire, November, p130.

Goux, D. and Zamora, P. (2001) 'La Formation en Entreprise Continue de se Développer'. *INSEE Première*, 759, February.

Klarsfeld, A. and Oiry, E. eds (2003) *Gérer les Competences: Des Instruments aux Processus*, Paris: Vuibert.

Labruyère, C., Paddeu, J., Savoyant, A., Teissier, J. and Rivoire, B. (2003) 'The Accreditation of Prior Learning in France: Review of Current Practices, Issues for Future Measures'. *Training and Employment*, Céreq, January – March. Available at http://www.cereq.fr/cereq/trai50.pdf.

Lenoir, H. (1996) 'Fonction Publique et Formation: Approche Comparative'. *Actualité de la Formation Permanente*, 140 pp15 – 22.

Lowezanin, C. and Perez, C. (2002) 'La Formation des Agents de la Fonction Publique: Exploitation de l'Enquête Formation Continue 2000'. Rapport pour l'Instance d'Évaluation de la Politique de Formation Continue des Agents de l'Etat. Commissariat Général du Plan, Paris, January, p87. Available at www.evaluation.gouv.fr/cgp/.

Marsick, V. J. and Watkins, K. E. (1999) *Facilitating Learning Organizations: Making Learning Count*, Aldershot: Gower.

Méhaut, P. (1995) 'The French System of Training Levies and the Dynamics of the Wage Earning Relationship'. *International Contribution to Labour Studies*, 5 pp115 – 29.

———— (2003) 'What Is the Future of Continuing Vocational Training? The Difficult Evolution of the French System'. ESCR seminar on Vocational Education, Warwick, September.

———— (2004) 'Competencies Based Management in Europe: What Consequences for the Labour Markets?'. *Economia et Lavoro*, September, forthcoming.

Merle, V. (2004) 'L'Accord Interprofessionnel du 20/09/2003 Relatif à l'Accès des Salariés à la Formation Tout au Long de la Vie: Un Accord Historique?'. *Droit Social*, forthcoming.

Perez, C. (2002) 'Continuing Training in the Public Service'. *Training and Employment* 48:July — September. Available at www.cereq.fr/cereq/training.html.

———— (2003) 'La Formation des Agents de la Fonction Publique au Miroir du Secteur Privé'. *Formation Emploi*, 81 pp81 – 97.

Vallemont, S. (1999) 'Gestion des Ressources Humaines dans l'Administration'. Rapport au Ministre de la Fonction Publique, de la Réforme de l'Etat et de la Décentralisation. Paris: La Documentation Française, p115.

COMMUNICATING CULTURE CHANGE

HRM implications for public sector organizations

Jennifer Waterhouse and Dianne Lewis

INTRODUCTION

Over the last three decades many public sector organizations have been the subject of large-scale changes frequently through the implementation of many private sector, managerialist philosophies aimed at increasing productivity, transparency and efficiency (Hood 1991; Osborne and Gaebler 1992). Many of these organizations have implemented practices such as sub-contracting, the creation of internal markets, local pay bargaining and performance-related pay (Doyle et al. 2000). Public sector organizations undergoing such reforms have experienced change greater than any in the private sector starting, as it was, from a traditional bureaucratic base, where services were provided based on social values and equity (Doyle et al. 2000). The cultures of public sector organizations however, have often been non-conducive to the implementation of such initiatives (O'Donnell 1998). In some cases the solution has therefore been to seek to change organizational cultures (Ferlie et al. 1996).

Culture change differs from other types of organizational change. The shared beliefs, values and behaviours of organizational members become the target of the change process rather than solely focusing on the structures and systems within which people work. What is sought is an alignment between human resource capabilities, systems and organizational structure so as better to achieve strategic organizational objectives (Beer et al. 1995). Within rapidly and continuously changing environments, such as that experienced in the public sector, it becomes critical that human resource capabilities are both aligned to the strategic objectives of the organization and that they are readily adaptable (Beer et al. 1995; Guest 1998; Nankervis et al. 1999).

Communication forms a fundamental aspect of such change (Eisenberg et al. 1999). Communication has predominantly been considered and researched as an 'instrument' within organizations, such as a conduit of information for achieving strategic goals (Lewis 1992; Putnam 1999). The magnitude of changes occurring within many public sector organizations makes the investigation of links between communication, culture and change of importance.

This article uses the Department of Main Roads, a large state government department in Queensland, Australia, as a case study for understanding the relationship between communication and change in a public sector department and the human resource implications of that relationship. Senior administrators of the department signalled their intention to change the culture of the department from one that was considered to be bureaucratic, technically oriented and inward-looking. The aim was to achieve a culture that was more outward-looking, adopting a philosophy of continual learning, more relationship oriented internally and inclusive of broader 'whole of government' objectives such as commercialization, the environment, social justice and community relations. The article considers the success achieved to date by using a communication model devised by Eisenberg et al. (1999) that theorizes the links between different types of communication and different types of organizational change.

The conclusions drawn in the article suggest that, despite an objective of shifting to a state of continual change with the mode of communication becoming dialogic, the communication mechanism faltered. This was due to a failure to address lower-level staff's need for a set vision and future direction, their perceptions of weaknesses in transformational leadership, inconsistencies and impreciseness in messages, a gap between messages and action and lack of communication between different areas of the department and with external stakeholders. These conclusions indicate that Human Resource Management is highly implicated in the change process in that employee motivation and commitment and, alignment between espoused values and organizational values is crucial to the success of organizational change efforts. The article addresses the limited investigation into communication and change within large, public sector organizations and considers some implications for theory. This includes how different forms of communication and change may simultaneously exist within organizations and the impact of context such as institutional environment, organizational size and complexity have on the ability to adopt different types of communication.

The article will give some background to the research at Main Roads, a brief explanation of relevant models of communication, culture and change, the methodology employed to obtain the findings, a discussion of the findings and implications for public sector organizations and theory.

BACKGROUND TO CHANGE AT MAIN ROADS

The last two decades in Australia, as in many countries, have been marked by a shift of philosophy in the public sector. Whereas prior to this time the relationship between the public sector and the community was based on the Weberian notion of consistent outcomes for consistent problems, public choice notions of improving productivity have significantly altered the relationship. This relationship between the public sector and the community has taken on a more marketplace approach where transactions are based not on equity but on notions of self-interest (Denhardt and Denhardt 2000). The adoption of market approaches to the delivery of government services, however, has been noted to consider insufficiently the public sector's role to 'serve and empower citizens' (Denhardt and Denhardt 2000: 549). This has resulted in members of public sector organizations needing to seek a balance between market approaches to the delivery of services and notions of citizenship inclusion.

Similar to many public sector organizations, the Department of Main Roads in Queensland has been faced with the challenges of both economic rationalism and citizen participation. Main Roads is a large state government department employing over 3,500 people across Queensland in both metropolitan and regional offices. While change is nothing new to Main Roads and its predecessor forms, which have been undergoing major changes in structure and orientation for over thirty years, most changes before 1996 were aimed only at efficiency. For example, in 1991 Main Roads became part of the mega-department of Queensland Transport (QT), and was then separated again from QT in 1996. The memory of the five years of amalgamation continues to rankle with Main Roads employees to this day who view this as a period of attempted cultural eradication.

Another example of changes for efficiency was the adoption of commercialization in the restructured Main Roads. The department was effectively split in two in a purchaser/provider arrangement resulting in approximately half the department now operating under predominantly commercial principles. The commercialized unit, RoadTek, competes for Main Roads (Corporate) projects with private sector construction companies and also receives guaranteed work to satisfy government employment objectives. This arrangement of both commercial and 'tied work' is in keeping with a public statement by the department in 1997 that 'Main Roads will invest in works of high priority, consistent with road investment strategies. Priority will be assessed by balancing both social and economic issues' (Wogan 1997: 2). Figure 1 provides a simplified organizational chart that summarizes the reporting lines and structure of the department. Of particular note is the level of geographic dispersion in both sides of the organization, but the more centralized reporting lines of RoadTek compared to that of the corporate arm.

The need to achieve greater citizenship participation objectives became critical for Main Roads following political fallout from a proposed major highway. While technically the proposal formed a sound solution to traffic problems, the plans did not sufficiently consider voter sentiment regarding the impact on a koala habitat. The resulting protest vote contributed to the ultimate downfall of the then Labour state government. A Labour government is again in office in Queensland and the ultimate survival of Main Roads as a separate entity from QT rests with its ability to be responsive to government and community.

To achieve greater responsiveness the focus has shifted from structural and system change to attempts to change the department's culture. Such change began in earnest in

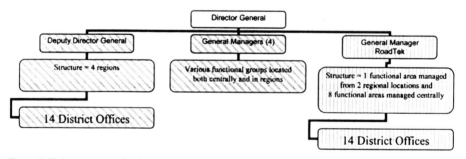

Figure 1: Main roads organizational chart and structure

1998 with the appointment of a new Director General. At this time a concerted effort was made to change the culture by the implementation of a change programme entitled 'The Three Frames', which encompassed, among other elements, a shift to a more relational way of doing business. The Three Frames management philosophy relies on three management systems working together simultaneously – alignment, relationships and achievement of a balanced performance scorecard. The main aim of the 'Alignment Frame' is to align people, systems and structures so that they work together for the achievement of the strategic plan. 'Relationships' means that Main Roads is to be based on genuine communication and information-sharing both internally and externally. The use of a 'Balanced Performance Scorecard' broadens the basis on which performance is to be measured. Performance previously had been measured in terms of financial and technical outcomes. The implementation of a Balanced Scorecard means that success is now to be considered in terms of customer/stakeholder relationships as well as good management of people and learning (Main Roads 1999).

The General Manager, Strategic Policy and Development, reiterated these sentiments in 1999 when he stated that, while Main Roads had a solid grounding in technical competence, they needed to do more than just build roads in order to maximize their contribution, their acceptance and their funding. They also needed to contribute to the government agenda, meet the needs of their own people, meet community needs, put in a solid financial performance, as *well* as build roads.

In the Annual Report of Main Roads, 1998 – 9, the Director General stated:

> Changing community and government expectations demanded Main Roads look critically at itself over the last 12 months, to ensure we were effectively aligned to meet the needs and challenges of the 21st century. These challenges were addressed using the three interacting frames, a relational alignment of the balanced performance scorecard, to achieve organizational transformation.
>
> (Main Roads 1999: 5)

In 2000, the Director General and instigator of the Three Frames Approach was transferred to a larger state government department. The incoming Director General, a Main Roads employee for over thirty years, pledged to continue the changes begun by his predecessor and to continue them through the introduction of five change themes as supporting strategies for the Three Frames. These strategies are represented as Five Signposts.

1. *Listening* to government, community, stakeholders and the private sector as well as to internal staff;
2. *Aligning* with government priorities, community priorities and the directions of road stewardship and construction maintenance as well as internal alignment in Main Roads;
3. *Leading* from the technical and professional basis, leading in implementing government and community needs where Main Roads leadership is appropriate and contributing to the leadership of agencies in the delivery of their outcomes;

4. *Positioning* Main Roads to be relevant, future focused and an integral part of public sector delivery on behalf of government to community and a strategic partner with the private sector;

5. *Learning* from activities, capturing those learnings and retaining corporate knowledge through initiatives like the Leadership and Learning Centre, managing organizational and individual management performance.

(Main Roads 2000: 5)

These five change themes sought to build organizational capabilities that were essential to taking practical action to address the challenges facing the department, particularly the challenge of being asked to do more with less (Internal Memorandum 2 March 2001). A key capability identified for success in meeting these challenges was improving the adaptiveness and change readiness of both departmental leaders and the departmental workforce (Internal Newsletter March 2001). The change process was therefore aimed at altering the human resource capabilities of the department as well as shifting the change impetus from a top–down planned approach to one more encompassing of ideals of continuous learning and continuous change.

While the establishment of excellent communication skills was an end-goal of the cultural change process, communication also formed an essential element of the change process itself. The primary target of the change process was an alteration in the human resource capabilities of the department. That is, the changes sought to develop capabilities within the department consistent with and capable of achieving the new strategic objectives. These include contributing to the government agenda, meeting the needs of staff, meeting community needs and achieving a solid financial performance. Culture, change and communication therefore become the focus of attention.

MODELS OF CULTURE, CHANGE AND COMMUNICATION

Models of organizational culture and change

Culture is generally considered to be the shared feelings, beliefs, values, attitudes, assumptions and behaviour among organizational members (Schein 1983, 1984, 1985). Early research on organizational culture was confined to the corporate sector and was prescriptive in its approach. Literature has followed many paths since culture first took managers' interest with Peters and Waterman's claim that a strong culture with particular attributes was the key to organizational success (Peters and Waterman 1982). Despite decades of academic debate, there remains little consensus on the nature of culture, its effects or how (if at all) it can be changed.

According to Chin and Benne (1973, 1976), there are three groups of strategies available to effect change. Empirical – rational (sometimes called 'cognitive') strategies assume that people are rational and will change their behaviour when they are given information showing them the changes are in their own best interest. Normative — re-educative strategies attempt to create a symbolic environment that people can relate to; these rely on shared meanings and symbolism and equate roughly to the 'culture' approach. And power — coercive strategies that emphasize political and economic sanctions. The problem is that normative — re-educative and power — coercive strategies are incompatible; 'the use of power strategies weakens any normative strategies' (Lewis 1992: 54). Additionally, these strategies for change are silent on the potential for bottom—up rather than top—down change.

Indeed, most early models of culture change were unitarist and biased in favour of managers. Including employees in the change process has only been significantly considered in recent times, though a 'supportive model' of change, which works on participation and joint co-operation between leaders and employees, had been put forward by Likert over forty years ago (Likert 1961). The application of supportive models to culture change arose from the association between Organization Development (OD) and transformational leadership. OD is a model of slow, planned change that concentrates on organizational effectiveness and employee well-being. Coupled with transformational leadership, culture change occurs through non-coercive, participative strategies. The model arising from this association considers culture change a long-term, non-coercive process in which organizational members willingly change their feelings, beliefs, values and behaviour through the forceful personality of a transformational leader (Bennis 1986; Tichy and Devanna 1986; Kuhnert and Lewis 1987; Avolio et al. 1991). The concept of transformational leadership has changed recently to include coercive means such as the power strategies suggested by Chin and Benne (1973, 1976) during the 'action stage' of change (Dunphy and Stace 1988; Lewis 1996).

As yet, few empirical studies have been carried out on the success of transformations whose 'action stage' consists almost solely of power-coercive strategies by management. However, with the current interest in transformational leadership and the push to achieve quality, re-engineering and knowledge management, some authors are beginning to advocate coercion as a legitimate primary strategy for change under some circumstances. Dunphy and Stace, for example, consider coercion as a strategy for use when time is short, support for change is low, but radical change is necessary for the organization's survival (Dunphy and Stace 1988, 1991; Stace and Dunphy 1994).

A problem with researching culture and culture change in the public sector is that historically culture's relevance and consequences were considered only for the private (profit-making) sector. However, the culture concept found its way from the private to the public sector in Australia from the findings of the Public Sector Review Committee (1987). The findings of the review acted as a major catalyst for change in the Queensland state public sector through the implementation of its recommendations that the public sector move towards a much more business-like approach to operating. The concern for public sector organizations is that, according to Deal and Kennedy (1988), culture change is a costly and time-consuming exercise.

The difficulties in effecting culture change are compounded through the observation that in any large organization, there is not one culture, but many sub-cultures (Gregory 1983; Martin and Siehl 1983; van Maanen and Barley 1985). According to Krefting and Frost, 'large numbers of heterogeneous subcultures make communication difficult, because communication is based on shared meanings' (1985: 157). Single-loop learning, which aims for behaviour change rather than complete culture change, may be easier to achieve and may also suffice. Most authors, including Schlesinger and Balzer (1985) and Arogyaswamy and Byles (1987), believe that behaviour is the only thing that affects performance – and culture is not the only determinant of behaviour. In cases where the aim is for second order change, the focus of enquiry becomes how such changes are implemented and how change messages are communicated through large, complex organizations.

Models of communication

Early models of communication such as the 1949 Shannon – Weaver model (in Griffin 1997) considered communication as a means of sending information from one place to another, with the aims being efficiency and effectiveness (Figure 2). Katz and Kahn (1967) extended this basic model of communication to represent an organization as an *open system*, with the *feedback* of information helping maintain or adjust the system.

These views of communication as an instrument and a conduit of information are still useful and were used in the early stages of the change process at Main Roads. The Katz and Kahn and Shannon and Weaver models do, however, assume one-way communication and that change is a specific event with both a starting point and planned end state. Later models of communication such as Lewis's 1987 model considered communication as a complex open system itself, but still did not consider the relationship between communication and change, or how modes of communication may need to change when change becomes continuous.

In their model, Eisenberg *et al.* (1999: 134) addressed the broader aspects of communication and drew together ideas of both organizational change and communication. Their model shows the relationships between different types of communication and different types of organizational change (Figure 3).

Eisenberg *et al.* (1999) identify that a significant problem with earlier change models is that they do not adequately consider the change needs of organizations in current times. In particular they note that many organizations today face the necessity of not just altering the way they operate, but completely changing the organization's goals and purpose. This requires a different style of change, a different role for leadership and different forms of communication. The main principle of their theory is that, the further we proceed away from the more traditional concept of change as a specific event and towards change as a continuing, learning experience, the more

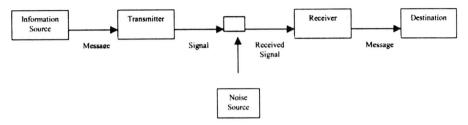

Figure 2: Shannon–Weaver model of communication

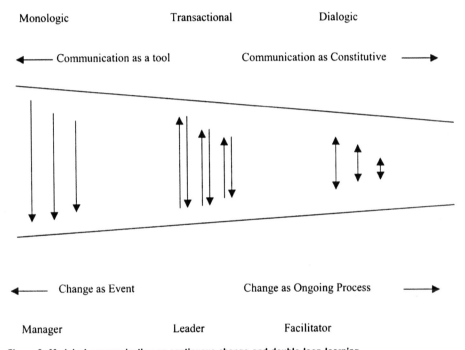

Figure 3: Model of communication as continuous change and double-loop learning

communication develops into dialogue and through dialogue, the achievement of double-loop learning. The traditional view of change as a specific event is therefore depicted at the left of Figure 3 where communication is one-way (monologic) and change is directed by a strong leader. An interim state is the transactional approach where leaders maintain a leadership role, but encourage employee participation. To achieve change that is radical and frame-breaking however requires the form of change and communication depicted at the right of the figure. This approach is where change is continual through double-loop learning and 'communication is constitutive of meaning' (Eisenberg *et al*. 1999: 134). Since double-loop learning is a stated goal of senior administrators of Main Roads, the model is considered appropriate for researching the relationship between communication and change in that department.

METHODOLOGY

The research methodology adopted was a case study, conducted using qualitative methods, in particular focus groups and individual interviews. The study of culture in organizations has had a long history in the qualitative research paradigm (Pettigrew 1979, 1997; Lewis 1995). This tradition has been founded on the basis that culture is a matter of human perception (Lewis 1995: 32). The methodological approach needed, therefore, was one capable of uncovering these perceptions (Brower *et al*. 2000). Focus groups were used to gather data from middle to lower-level employees for three main reasons. First, culture was identified as a shared phenomenon, existing within groups (Hofstede 1998). Focus groups therefore provided the opportunity to observe the interaction of individuals within their own working groups (Morgan 1988). Second, focus groups gave participants the opportunity to comment on what they felt was most important rather than their being prompted by an interviewer (Krueger 1994; Morrison 1998). This was considered particularly important for lower-level staff where there may have been a view of power imbalance between the researcher and the researched. Third, the use of focus groups allowed for the efficient collection of greater quantities of rich data than would have been achievable through one-on-one interviews (Morgan 1988). This was particularly important given the geographic distribution of the department. To gain geographical coverage focus groups were conducted with metropolitan groups located within the state's capital, employees located within larger regional centres and employees located in smaller, remote sites.

Senior officers within the department were interviewed using a semi-structured format. The decision to use this method of data collection was two-fold. First, it excluded senior officers from focus groups where their presence may have interfered with the readiness of junior staff to contribute. Second, given senior staff's role as instigators, and in some cases both instigators and recipients of change, it was important to gain their perceptions of what changes they were seeking to implement, as well as their perceptions of what the most senior management in the department were seeking to achieve. Semi-structured interviews were considered the most suitable method of achieving this, as they allowed the main topics and general themes to be targeted through specific questions while also allowing the freedom to pursue other relevant issues as they arose (Maykut and Morehouse 1994).

The research was conducted at four discrete time periods over a period of two-and-a-half years commencing with the collection of base line data in August 2000. The data collection process was then replicated as closely as possible in the next three rounds.

Table 1 outlines the timing, number of focus groups and participants at each time-frame.

Rather than achieve proportional representation, focus group participants were purposefully selected from volunteers within the department to give as broad a spread of perspectives as possible. That is, the aim was not to achieve proportional representation but rather a horizontal and vertical slice of the organization with representation achieved at as many levels, geographical locations and across as broad a range of job classifications as possible. To ensure a cross-section of the population was obtained, demographics were collected of each participant at each focus group, including age, gender, occupational stream, employment level and length of employment.

An adaptive approach to data collection was adopted, similar to that proposed by Layder (1998). As the research was undertaken, further data sources were identified as important to the process of change within the organization. These sources were pursued and included further interviews with key individuals, the attendance by researchers at internal conferences and seminars, as well as referral to both internal and public documents. The various sources were used to strengthen the reliability of the data through triangulation. Validity was also aided by returning summaries of focus group findings to participants to ensure that the researchers' interpretation faithfully represented the views of organizational members.

FINDINGS AND DISCUSSION

As the research was conducted in four stages over a period of two-and-a-half years (2000 – 2), findings varied from one round of interviews and focus groups to the next. This section details findings from round 1 (August – September 2000), rounds 2 and 3 (March – June 2001 and October – December 2002) and round 4 (April – May 2002), highlighting specific findings in regard to communication during those periods.

Table 1: Time-frame of data collection

Round	Date	Number of focus groups	Number of participants
1	August – September 2000	18	150
2	March – June 2001	16	120
3	October – December 2001	14	94
4	April – May 2002	15	104

Round 1 (August – September 2000)

Initially the change initiative took the form of a planned, top – down approach, with change communicated from the senior management ranks to the bottom of the organization, characteristic of Shannon and Weaver's 1949 transmission model of communication. Communication was therefore monologic and change seen as an event towards the specific end of a more relational culture (Eisenberg et al. 1999). It was envisioned that the Three Frames approach would filter from the top of the organization through management ranks to the bottom. There was an expectation that the need for the change to a more relational culture would be accepted as a logical necessity to avoid re-amalgamation with Queensland Transport. Therefore, the strategy employed represented a combination of empirical-rational and normative-re-educative (Chin and Benne 1973, 1976). It was realized, however, that blockages in communication were occurring:

> It took Jim (Director General) 18 months before he realized this (filtering) had not happened as well as he thought it would. He called his guys together and he said 'how is it going?' and they would say 'yeah fine'. But when they were telling their troops, they still weren't confident with it (the Three Frames) or totally understanding of it.
>
> (Focus Group comment)

The response to this disjointed communication was the Director General intervening to communicate directly to staff the new strategic direction of the organization and the changes to human resource capabilities required to achieve those strategic objectives. At the time, the Director General commented that he had traversed the state seeking to understand the organization's culture, relationships and alignment issues. His personal representation therefore offered an avenue through which feedback from staff could be encompassed into the change process suggesting a more transactional approach to communication. The Director General continued to use a combination of empirical-rational and normative-re-educative strategies with staff, but within the senior management ranks a more power-coercive strategy was adopted to gain support for the organization's new direction. The Director General, in interview, commented that he sought direction from senior managers, but at the same time offered exit strategies to those who did not wish to be involved in the change agenda.

It was considered then that strong leadership had been responsible for the strategic changes occurring in the organization and that, on the change of Director General, the commitment of the new leadership would be an essential element in any future changes. Round 1 interviews and focus groups therefore identified the importance of transformational leadership and the communication of a clear vision in successfully undertaking cultural change within organizations. This part of the change process therefore most closely reflected change as an event, mainly monologic communication and strong leadership as depicted in the left of Eisenberg *et al.*'s (1999) model (Figure 2).

Staff in focus groups expressed concern at the increase in workloads that the changes had brought. In particular, expectations relating to processes such as communication and consultation with external stakeholders were seen as adding significantly to both the cost and workloads associated with the preliminary stages of road construction projects. Despite this, there appeared limited resistance regarding the direction of change and there was broad acceptance that the decided strategic direction should be set, communicated and driven from the top of the organization, down. A divisional employee commented: 'I think it's going to require incredible leadership to not stop the pendulum from just swinging back to the status quo, from everyone going back to saying, oh that's good, that's comfortable.'

While there were differences in the extent to which different parts of the organization adopted change, there was broad agreement that it was acceptable for culture change and strategic direction to be coercively communicated and driven from the top. Dialogue was confined to at-level or within specific organizational groups and the focus on communication differed in various parts of the organization. This difference was particularly marked between Corporate and RoadTek regional offices. Corporate offices tended to focus on communication between themselves and their head office whereas RoadTek's primary concern was on communication and relationships with the Corporate offices located within their local area. It was suggested by RoadTek staff that the corporate arm had not embraced change to the same degree as the commercialized arm and that this was causing communication tensions between the two groups. This suggests that while dialogue was occurring, the culture of the organization at this time did not support open dialogue from the bottom to the top or that dialogue across the organization should form part of the strategic change process.

Such cultural limitations were evidenced in the response to Main Roads Junction. Main Roads Junction is an electronic means of communication between offices and, in particular, between Corporate regional offices and head office. The system is mainly used for the transmission of messages concerning policy, structural, technical, operational and personnel changes; but both commercial and RoadTek staff in the regions said that only those employees with sufficient time, interest and resources accessed the available information. There was no acknowledgement of the system's capabilities in regard to feedback. Likewise, email was considered problematic. Both Corporate regional and RoadTek staff expressed concern that head office was unsympathetic to their high workloads and expected immediate responses to email requests. The hesitancy for staff to use email as a means to express their concerns further confirmed that communication, particularly between regional offices and head office, remained firmly monologic.

Both Corporate and RoadTek regional offices were also resistant to interference by Corporate head office in the operational side of their businesses. There was a call for greater consultation prior to the implementation of new operational systems and guidelines. Given the strategic emphasis on building relationships, there was a sense that management was failing to *walk the talk* when they failed to consult on operational changes. Paradoxically, there was little resistance or concern among organizational members of the coercive strategies being used to achieve cultural change. Nor was there recognition of the incongruence of such strategies with the 'relational' culture the organization was seeking to espouse. At the non-strategic level, therefore, staff were demanding a greater say in decisions that affected their daily working lives and that, for such changes, a more transactional mode of communication was deemed desirable. This suggests multiple communication and change styles occurring simultaneously within the one organization.

Overall, the consistent theme throughout the department was that Main Roads needed to be more proactive in nurturing relationships and in creating opportunities for staff to participate in low-level decision making. They needed to improve communication with the regions and to consult with them more. At the same time, however, there was also a general acceptance of strategic change directed from the top and the need for strong leadership to move the organization forward. As Main Roads began the communication of culture change as top–down, one-way and as a specific event, the *elements* contained within the Shannon–Weaver, Katz and Kahn and Lewis models are applicable to the early stages of the change programme. There was evidence also of growing expectations in consultation suggesting a limited shift to more transactional modes of communication.

Rounds 2 and 3 (March–June and October–December 2001)

Main themes reported on during the second and third rounds of interviews and discussions varied little from those reported on in the first round; that is, leadership, workloads, communication and the uneven diffusion of change throughout the organization. However, a significant difference between the first round and the second and third rounds was the growing impatience with the change strategies being used. While most people were able to excuse any flaws in strategies in the early stages of the change process, they were now beginning to become disillusioned as to whether the processes would improve. During rounds 2 and 3, therefore, the main concerns within Main Roads related to leaders, their behaviour and their communication style.

There was a perception that the communication of the changes was progressing so randomly and at such a rapid pace that the department was under threat of losing efficiencies and that communication and diffusion of change throughout the organization was becoming more fractured and uneven. These perceptions were accompanied by reports of a reduction in the visibility of the Director General. Whereas in round 1 it was considered that strong leadership was driving the changes, in round 2 the leadership of change from the top of the organization was considered to have faltered. While the current Director General introduced the Five Signposts with the intention of their being complementary to the Three Frames, these additions served only to blur the original direction and were perceived by lower-level staff as communication 'noise'. There was therefore growing uncertainty as to what Main Roads would look like in the future.

Focus groups and interview participants also identified a lack of unity in the senior management team, which was at odds with the messages of a 'relational' approach to work processes. Within the Senior Management Group (SMG) there was some expectation that the cultural change would now be sufficient to shift the organization towards continual change and double-loop learning. Instead, the attempted shift to dialogue appeared to be too rapid and sufficient time had not been given to the interim transactional step necessary to develop more open lines of communication. Transactional communication involves continued strong leadership (Eisenberg et al. 1999) and staff within the department continued to place reliance on leader guidance.

Within Main Roads there exist different sub-cultures within the senior management group itself, between Main Roads and its external environment, between head office and the regions and between the commercial and corporate arms. The different sub-cultures within the SMG began to be more readily identified and the perceived divisions within the SMG caused concern among organizational members at this time. Staff believed the SMG was experiencing relational problems/breakdowns, which were culminating in divisions between different directors and their working units, creating a silo mentality and causing a loss of strategic direction. It was considered that this apparent loss of a defined and unified strategic direction was resulting in increased reporting requests as senior management sought direction from regional offices. Because the SMG were not communicating among themselves, it was considered that requests for information were uncoordinated and often duplicated.

Regional staff expressed frustration that the extra work created by the increased reporting requirements was not being rewarded as there appeared little evidence that their recommendations were being acted upon. One regional focus group commented that sometimes the best course of action was not taken because the department suffered from a 'seniority complex', where consultation happened, but advice was always taken from senior levels rather than from the staff that the changes impacted directly upon. This view is distinctive from that noted in round 1. Rather than communication mechanisms being seen as a means for head office to deliver monologic direction to regions, there was now growing expectation that these mechanisms provided the means through which a more transactional mode of communication could be developed. However, the complexities created by the existence of sub-cultures both at the senior management level and across the organization were beginning to more seriously impact on communication channels (Krefting and Frost 1985). Whereas in the first round this was manifest in communication at-level and within professional groups, in round 2 the existence of sub-cultures began to act as a barrier across hierarchical levels. Rather than order emerging from chaos (Eisenberg et al. 1999) sub-cultures stood as a barrier to the adoption of more transactional communication or the establishment of true dialogue. The result was that the change processes commenced under the previous Director General were stalling.

Simultaneously, there was a view that the department was becoming more bureaucratic. A sentiment on leadership from one metropolitan focus group was that the department was becoming more 'authoritarian' with regard to approval processes. Management style was referred to as 'control and command' and another focus group commented that 'some distrust has been caused by head office forcing change on the regional offices and having systems fail to do the job required'. Expectations regarding consultation had therefore been established, but leadership style was seen as contradictory to the establishment of dialogue.

Decision-making processes, resource allocation and communication between units were therefore considered problematic. It was proposed that the SMG should be more honest and authentic in their dealings and relationships to demonstrate the transparency needed to progress the change process, and that middle management would continue to experience problems relating to staff until the SMG corrected their behaviours. Considering Eisenberg *et al.*'s (1999) model, the main issues in rounds 2 and 3 were a mismatch between leadership style, staff expectations and the mode of change preferred by leaders and followers within the organization.

Round 4 (April – May 2002)

Findings from this final round of data collection indicated a growing divide between corporate and commercial arms. When focus group questions to RoadTek staff were couched in terms that referred to 'Main Roads', there appeared some confusion as to whether this term referred to them. While they acknowledged the authority of the SMG and Director General, they identified increasingly with their own Director. An implication of this was that in setting strategic direction, RoadTek employees appeared more empowered and less hampered by political considerations. There was some acknowledgement that ultimate political decisions in regard to RoadTek's future such as corporatization or privatization remained in the hands of government, while others felt that through being successful at what they did they would be in a position of power better to negotiate their own future and have input into the process. RoadTek's flatter structure resulted in a far greater awareness and ownership of their own strategic direction, which they often viewed as distinct and separate from that of the remainder of Main Roads. Despite considerable geographic dispersion, RoadTek focus group participants were able to quote almost verbatim the messages of their Director and were very clear on their positions and roles.

RoadTek perceived that it had, in the main, shifted to a more transactional mode of communication and considered itself more adaptable than the corporate arm. Lines of communication between lower-level staff in RoadTek and their senior management were considered more open and less susceptible to 'noise' than that of their corporate counterparts suggesting that hierarchically, at least, the mode of communication within RoadTek was becoming more transactional. This was remarkable given that during this period RoadTek instigated a number of major structural and system changes, including a planned diminishment in the number of regions from four to two. RoadTek therefore appeared to have shifted along the continuum towards dialogue and something more closely approaching a culture of continuous change than their *corporate cousins*. Corporate, on the other hand, talked about the filtering of messages as they cascaded from the top and reported a sense that many changes were 'imposed', suggesting that Corporate remained fixed at the one-way, monologic end of the communication spectrum and that change remained a series of 'events' rather than an ongoing process.

Furthermore, despite the formal release of the strategic plan, Corporate staff both in regions and head office felt that there was a continued lack of strategic direction and a continuing gap between leadership words and actions. This was blamed on a tightening budgetary environment that resulted in a lack of decision making by senior management. According to one focus group, 'Because the only news they (SMG) can give is bad news, they are not giving any news at all.' What is of interest here is the view of growing authority accompanied by a perceived diminution of messages regarding change despite the release of the strategic plans. This suggests a mismatch between leader communication of change contained within the strategic plans and the mode of transmission expected and needed by staff. Again the reliance was on normative – re-educative strategies (Chin and Benne 1973, 1976) by natural cascading throughout the organization.

Communication between the two arms of the department increased but was conflictual. RoadTek believed that Corporate was not fully conversant with or appreciative of the financial imperatives under which they operated and Corporate felt RoadTek were becoming arrogant. Eisenberg *et al.* (1999) suggest that dialogic communication such as this can lead to transformation. At the time data collection ceased, there was growing evidence of this possibility. Sub-cultures, while adding to the complexity of communication, were showing some evidence of learning from one another. However, this did not appear necessarily to align with the direction set by the SMG.

The continuing lack of both message clarity and of consultation about change within Corporate resulted in a feeling of disengagement from the change process. One head office group saw this within the corporate arm as a specific outcome of a shift back to a more hierarchical framework with defined chains of command. More positively, however, many groups perceived better relationships and communication within their own offices. This was seen as an outcome of measures aimed at implementing a team culture that resulted in improved sharing of information and greater interaction between work units. A negative of this, however, was the sense that some hid behind their teams and no one took responsibility for their own actions.

There was also a general feeling that a lot of the change processes had been the direct result of external influences and that the department was taking on a reactive role rather than being proactive in its change initiatives. One regional group reported however, that change was now coming from the coalface rather than being driven from the top. This suggests some promising shift in ideas about communication and changes in Main Roads and may represent a positive move towards a more sustainable continuous change initiative using genuine dialogue as an impetus. However, it also raises an under-investigated aspect of continuous change processes – the impact of pressures outside organizational boundaries and how and at what point they interact with organizational members within continuous change models. Whereas power-coercive strategies have increasingly been used in times of external threat (Dunphy and Stace 1988, 1991; Stace and Dunphy 1994), models of continuous change appear silent on this issue.

SUMMATION

Communication as either a conduit of change or as a means through which members re-construct the organization appears problematic in this case. Where communication is considered as a conduit of change, some staff felt a sense of over-communication and too much information from some quarters; others stated a lack of communication and consultation. Issues such as the filtering of messages between head office and lower-level staff by middle management formed a significant blockage to the communication of strategic direction as did uncoordinated and duplicated requests for information. Therefore there continues to be some confusion among staff over the future strategic direction of Main Roads. It was claimed that change was still being driven from the top without appropriate communication and discussion about work expectations and the practicability of those expectations. This overload of information and requests for information has resulted in a distortion of the messages being received about strategic direction.

In Shannon and Weaver's 1949 model of communication (in Griffin 1997), communication is viewed as a one-way process from information source through transmitter to receivers and the final destination. Within this process is the potential for disruption of message transmittal through 'noise'. In the case of Main Roads, the transmittal and receipt of strategic messages evidenced four sources of very serious 'noise'. First, in what was understood to be an environment of shrinking budgets, many people were unable to reconcile the growing expenditure on consultation when this was matched by cuts in the amount for actual construction. Second, there was a sense that senior decision-makers within the department were more ready to accept the advice of external stakeholders and consultants than utilize the expert resources already contained within the department. This was considered to be contrary to ideas of participation and internal relationships. Third, the opportunity for lower-level employees to adopt a more relational way of work depends significantly upon their immediate supervisors and/or middle management. Fourth, regions in particular continued to report heavy workloads and long working hours at odds with Main Roads' stated objective. The entrenched *hero mentality* within the department continues to equate working longer hours with being a good worker and climbing up the corporate ladder suggesting little cultural change in this respect.

The conclusions on communication in Main Roads suggest that, despite an objective of shifting to a state of continual change where the mode of communication would be anticipated as dialogic, the communication mechanism faltered due to lower-level staff's need for a set vision and future direction, their perceptions of weaknesses in transformational leadership, inconsistencies and impreciseness in messages, a gap between messages and action and lack of communication between different areas of the department.

IMPLICATIONS FOR HUMAN RESOURCE MANAGEMENT WITHIN PUBLIC SECTOR ORGANIZATIONS

The concepts of culture and culture change and the combination of commercialization with greater citizen participation within the public sector are relatively recent phenomena. The case study of Main Roads may therefore provide valuable insights for other government departments, both in Australia and in other parts of the world, as they seek to balance satisfying stakeholder needs with concepts of economic rationalism and its manifestation, commercialization.

The article has concentrated on the issue of communication as it seems that, for culture change to succeed, communication as a conduit of information has to evolve into dialogue and through dialogue, double-loop learning. If organizational culture is indeed internal feelings, beliefs, values and basic assumptions about work (Schein 1983, 1984, 1985), and if public sector organizations genuinely want culture change (double-loop learning) rather than merely behaviour change (single-loop learning), Eisenberg *et al.*'s model (1999) suggests that people should not simply be responding to instructions from the top of the organization, but should be a genuine part of a dialogic process. In the case presented here it would appear that there has been only limited movement in that direction and little consideration by organizational members of the relative values of monologic and dialogic communication, or behaviour and culture change.

For Main Roads, the main aim of the change was for the department to become more relational and responsive to external stakeholder needs. The aligning of the human resource capabilities of the department with this strategic goal included a reconfiguration of the focus of the department. The aim was to achieve not just technical and financial outcomes, but also human oriented ones including improved relationships with both external and internal stakeholders. That is, as the department became more relationally focused externally there was an expectation that relationships within the department would also improve to align with its new strategic objectives. These relationships would be supported through open, dialogic style communication. There was no expectation within Main Roads that such dialogue would be congenial and Eisenberg *et al.*'s (1999) model does not propose this. Indeed, the model suggests conflict, rather than congeniality, as a means of continuous change.

The most significant implication for public sector management emerging from this study, therefore, is the extent to which true dialogic communication is achievable, or indeed desirable. Often within public sector organizations the main impetus for change is political, usually in the form of an external threat. This was the case with Main Roads through the political fallout from the 'koala road' and a political agenda to re-merge Main Roads with Queensland Transport. Under circumstances of external threat, where the need for change is urgent, leaders have used coercive means to change quickly their organizations (Dunphy and Stace 1988). In setting the strategic direction of Main Roads and the necessity for rapid change, there was little time for dialogic debate. Indeed, evidence from the case study suggests that there was general acceptance, at least within the corporate division of the department, that the Director General held legitimate power to interpret ministerial needs and enforce a specific strategic direction. Under circumstances of political stress, where the need for change is urgent, it does not appear desirable to enter into two-way strategies for change or entertain the dialogic communication associated with such change. Findings from this research suggest that while dialogic communication regarding day-to-day operational activities is desirable to lower-level staff there is also an appreciation of the limitations of this approach when applied to the demands of political leaders.

Where there may be further tensions with this finding is with hybrid organizational structures within public sector organizations such as the commercial and corporate arms of Main Roads. Purchaser/provider arrangements such as these are a common New Public Management initiative. An implication for public sector management emerging from this study is the difficulty of communication between different arms of large and complex departments, because each arm has its own sub-culture. Interestingly, in the case of Main Roads, the development of a 'team culture' was said to have created better relationships and communication within the teams, but not necessarily across teams. The implication of this is that it may not be possible to develop a 'one department' culture aligned to strategic objectives. Rather than attempting to create a mono-culture with the focus on relationships between individuals, the focus instead becomes managing the communication channels between the disparate sub-cultures to ensure that they understand how their roles contribute to the overall strategic plan.

The differences identified between the corporate and commercial arms of Main Roads illustrate the need to consider how leadership and organizational structure, especially where that structure remains strongly hierarchical, impact on an organization's ability to enter into true dialogue and therefore achieve continuous change. Public sector organizations seeking a culture of continuous change may require considerable structural change. The indications from this case study suggest that fewer hierarchical organizational levels as well as a hands-on style leader are more conducive to dialogue and continuous change. The challenge will be to manage the expectations of dialogue among organizational members when decisions need to be enacted rapidly and without consultation.

RoadTek's perception of empowerment and lack of being hampered by political considerations may be illusory, however, having established some expectation of dialogue it may be difficult to draw this back and successfully implement change from the top. This becomes particularly problematic when employees demand input into strategic decision-making processes. Having established an expectation of consultation, the use of power-coercive strategies to implement future organizational change may fall on very unfertile ground, resulting in a protracted and painful change process. If the goal is to create public sector organizations conducive to continuous change, and if continuously changing organizations are associated with genuine dialogue, the issue for government is whether political exigencies are able to wait for such dialogue to occur. It is also an issue as to whether the outcomes of such dialogue provide government with politically palatable solutions. Therefore, there is a place for both dialogue and power – coercive strategies to enact change within public sector organizations, however the challenge becomes how to move between the two.

IMPLICATIONS FOR THEORY AND CONCLUSION

Main Roads, Queensland, Australia, is but one case of a large, public sector organization undergoing change, and the findings may not all be universally transferable. However, according to Eisenhardt, 'theory developed from case study research is likely to have important strengths like novelty, testability, and empirical evidence' (1989: 548). It is also well suited to 'new research areas or research areas for which existing theory seems inadequate' (Eisenhardt 1989: 549). Only limited research has to date been undertaken that considers specifically the communication aspects of large-scale change in public sector organizations.

There are some implications for theory emerging from this case, and some areas for future research. First, Eisenberg et al.'s (1999) model (Figure 3) is useful in considering how organizations may move from monologic to dialogic communication, but is silent on how organizations may shift back. The case of Main Roads indicates that, not only may it be necessary for this to occur, but that different types of communication were able to co-exist at different levels within the organizations and for different change purposes. Strategic directives that impact across large, complex organizations, especially when these are in response to external threat, seem most suited to monologic direction. Below the strategic level, dialogue, particularly between different functional areas, appears capable of delivering change on a smaller scale. It is contended however, that dialogue can result in organizational transformation (Eisenberg *et al*. 1999). In the case of Main Roads, the result of leaving change to the forces of dialogue resulted in the diffusion of change becoming fractured and uneven, rather than dialogue being a force for organizational transformation. It appears that ultimately, some action must be taken to enact the changes agreed to if transformation is to occur. It may be argued that, given time transformation may ultimately have occurred through dialogue. Eisenberg *et al*.'s model however is silent on the issue of time and pace of change. Furthermore, while it is suggested that the possessors of power may 'disproportionately shape organizational symbols and meanings' (Eisenberg *et al*. 1999: 141) the issue that arises in geographically dispersed organizations is whose voices get heard and how are messages ultimately communicated to all organizational members to enact true transformation.

Institutional pressures are also not considered in the Eisenberg *et al*. model (1999) in that it relies primarily on communication within, rather than external, to organizations. Within the public sector, institutional changes such as those under New Public Management within the Anglo-western world, have been major forces for change. Externally driven decisions such as commercialization and purchaser/provider splits as in the case of Main Roads have significant effect on the construction of organizational meaning. The extent to which commercial imperatives changed the culture of RoadTek is testimony to this. An area for future research, in models of continuous change, is the investigation of how institutional changes interact with the dialogue of organizational members to bring about change through means other than leadership.

To conclude, Main Roads has led the way – in Australia, at least – in the attempted introduction of open communication in the public sector. While it is easy to find fault with their strategies and their methods, and while some of the results may be less than perfect and less successful than senior management would want, their efforts represent an experiment in open communication, both internal and external. Main Roads have tried to keep all staff informed of the transcendental, strategic and operational goals and activities of the organization; and they have openly shared information on these goals with other government departments. That represents a first in Australian public sector management.

REFERENCES

Arogyaswamy, B. and Byles, C. (1987) 'Organizational Culture: Internal and External Fits'. *Journal of Management Inquiry*, 13 pp647–59.

Avolio, B., Waldman, D. A. and Yammarino, F. J. (1991) 'Leading in the 1990s: The Four I's of Transformational Leadership'. *Journal of European Industrial Training (UK)*, 15:4 pp9–16.

Beer, M., Eisenstat, R. A. and Biggadike, E. R. (1995) 'Strategic Change: A New Dimension of Human Resource Management' in G. R. Ferris, S. D. Rosen and D. T. Barnum (eds) *Handbook of Human Resource Management*. Cambridge, MA: Blackwell Publishers.

Bennis, W. (1986) 'Transformative Power and Leadership' in T. J. Sergiovanni and J. E. Corbally (eds) *Leadership and Organizational Culture*. Chicago, IL: University of Illinois Press.

Brower, R. S., Abolafia, M. Y. and Carr, J. B. (2000) 'On Improving Qualitative Methods in Public Administration Research'. *Administration and Society*, 32:4 pp363 – 97.

Chin, R. and Benne, K. D. (1973) 'General Strategies for a Changing Organization' in S. J. Jun and W. B. Storm (eds) *Tomorrow's Organizations: Challenges and Strategies*. Glenview, IL: Scott, Foresman & Company.

———— (1976) 'General Strategies for Effecting Changes in Human Systems' in W. Bennis, K. Benne and R. Chin (eds) *The Planning of Change*. New York: Holt, Rinehart & Winston.

Deal, T. E. and Kennedy, A. A. (1988) *Corporate Cultures: The Rites and Rituals of Corporate Life*, London: Penguin Books.

Denhardt, R. B. and Denhardt, J. V. (2000) 'The New Public Service: Serving Rather Than Steering.' *Public Administration Review*, 60:6 pp549 – 59.

Doyle, M., Claydon, T. and Buchanan, D. (2000) 'Mixed Results, Lousy Process: The Management Experience of Organizational Change'. Special Issue of *British Journal of Management*, 11 ppS59 – S80.

Dunphy, D. C. and Stace, D. A. (1988) 'Transformational and Coercive Strategies for Planned Organisational Change: Beyond the OD Model'. *Organisation Studies*, 9/3:(c) 1988 EGOS pp317 – 34.

———— (1991) 'Strategies for Organisational Transition'. The Centre for Corporate Change Working Paper Series, CCC Paper No. 002.

Eisenberg, E. M., Andrews, L., Murphy, A. and Laine-Timmerman, L. (1999) 'Transforming Organizations through Communication' in P. Salem (ed.) *Organizational Communication and Change*. Cresskill, NJ: Hampton Press.

Eisenhardt, K. M. (1989) 'Building Theories from Case Study Reseach'. *Academy of Management Review*, 14:4 pp532 – 50.

Ferlie, E., Pettigrew, A., Ashburner, L. and Fitzgerald, L. (1996) *The New Public Management in Action*, Oxford: Oxford University Press.

Gregory, K. L. (1983) 'Native-View Paradigms: Multiple Cultures and Culture Conflicts in Organizations'. *Administrative Science Quarterly*, 28 pp359 – 76.

Griffin, E. M. (1997) *A First Look at Communication Theory*, New York: McGraw Hill.

Guest, D. E. (1998) 'Beyond HRM: Commitment and the Contract Culture' in P. Sparrow and M. Marchington (eds) *Human Resource Management: The New Agenda*. London: Financial Times Management.

Hofstede, G. (1998) 'Identifying Organisational Subcultures: An Empirical Approach'. *Journal of Management Studies*, 35:1 pp1 – 12.

Hood, C. (1991) 'A Public Management for All Seasons?'. *Public Administration*, 69:1 pp3 – 19.

Katz, D. and Kahn, R. (1967) *The Social Psychology of Organizations*, New York: Wiley.

Krefting, L. A. and Frost, P. J. (1985) 'Untangling Webs, Surfing Waves, and Wildcatting: A Multiple-Metaphor Perspective on Managing Organizational Culture' in P. J. Frost, L. F. Moore, M. R. Louis, C. C. Lundberg and J. Martin (eds) *Organizational Culture: The Meaning of Life in the Workplace*. Beverly Hills, CA: Sage Publications.

Krueger, R. A. (1994) *Focus Groups: A Practical Guide for Applied Research*, Thousand Oaks, CA: Sage Publications.

Kuhnert, K. W. and Lewis, P. (1987) 'Transactional and Transformational Leadership: A Constructive/Developmental Analysis'. *Academy of Management Review*, 12:4 pp648 – 57.

Layder, D. (1998) *Sociological Practice: Linking Theory and Social Research*, London: Sage Publications.

Lewis, D. (1995) 'Researching Strategic Change – Methodologies, Methods and Techniques' in D. E. Hussey (ed.) *Rethinking Strategic Management: Ways to Improve Competitive Performance*. Chichester: John Wiley & Sons.

Lewis, D. S. (1992) 'Communicating Organizational Culture'. *Australian Journal of Communication*, 19:2 pp47–57.

———— (1996) 'The Organizational Culture Saga – from OD to TQM: A Critical Review of the Literature. Part 2 - Applications'. *Leadership and Organization Development Journal*, 17:2 pp9–16.

Lewis, P. (1987) *Organizational Communication: The Essence of Effective Management*, New York: Wiley.

Likert, R. (1961) *New Patterns of Management*, New York: McGraw Hill.

Main Roads (1999) *Annual Report*, Brisbane: Department of Main Roads.

———— (2000) *Annual Report*, Brisbane: Department of Main Roads.

Martin, J. and Siehl, C. (1983) 'Organizational Culture and Counter-Culture: An Uneasy Symbiosis'. *Organizational Dynamics*, Autumn: 52–64.

Maykut, P. and Morehouse, R. (1994) *Beginning Qualitative Research: A Philosophic and Practical Guide*, London: The Falmer Press.

Morgan, D. L. (1988) *Focus Groups as Qualitative Research*, Newbury Park, CA: Sage Publications.

Morrison, D. E. (1998) *The Search for a Method: Focus Groups and the Development of Mass Communication Research*, Luton: University of Luton Press.

Nankervis, A. R., Compton, R. L. and McCarthy, T. E. (1999) *Strategic Human Resource Management*, South Melbourne: Nelson ITP.

O'Donnell, M. (1998) 'Creating a Performance Culture? Performance-Based Pay in the Australian Public Service'. *Australian Journal of Public Administration*, 57:3 pp28–40.

Osborne, D. and Gaebler, T. (1992) *Reinventing Government: How the Entrepreneurial Spirit Is Transforming the Public Sector*, Reading, MA: Addison-Wesley Publishing Company.

Peters, T. J. and Waterman, R. H. (1982) *In Search of Excellence*, New York: Harper & Row.

Pettigrew, A. M. (1979) 'On Studying Organizational Cultures'. *Administrative Science Quarterly*, 24:4 pp570–81.

———— (1997) 'What Is a Processual Analysis?'. *Scandinavian Journal of Management*, 13:4 pp338–48.

Public Sector Review Committee (1987) *Public Sector Review Report*, Brisbane: Queensland Government Printer.

Putnam, L. (1999) 'Shifting Metaphors of Organizational Communication: The Rise of Discourse Perspectives' in P. Salem (ed.) *Organizational Communication and Change*. Cresskill, NJ: Hampton Press.

Schein, E. H. (1983) 'The Role of the Founder in Creating Organizational Culture'. *Organizational Dynamics*, Summer pp13–28.

———— (1984) 'Coming to a New Awareness of Organizational Culture'. *Sloan Management Review*, Winter pp3–16.

———— (1985) *Organizational Culture and Leadership*, San Francisco, CA: Jossey-Bass.

Schlesinger, L. A. and Balzer, J. J. (1985) 'An Alternative to Buzzword Management: The Culture – Performance Link'. *Personnel*, September pp45–51.

Stace, D. A. and Dunphy, D. C. (1994) *Beyond the Boundaries: Leading and Re-creating the Successful Enterprise*, Sydney: McGraw Hill.

Tichy, N. and Devanna, M. (1986) 'The Transformational Leader'. *Training and Development Journal*, July pp27–32.

Van Maanen, J. and Barley, S. R. (1985) 'Cultural Organization: Fragments of a Theory' in P. J. Frost, L. F. Moore, M. R. Louis, C. C. Lundberg and J. Martin (eds) *Organizational Culture: The Meaning of Life in the Workplace*. Beverly Hills, CA: Sage Publications.

Wogan, D. (1997) 'Queensland Department of Main roads Southern Region Symposium'. Toowoomba, November.

WORK – LIFE BALANCE

Exploring the connections between levels of influence in the UK public sector

Gillian A. Maxwell and Marilyn McDougall

INTRODUCTION

Work – life balance (WLB) is defined by the UK Department of Trade and Industry as being 'about adjusting working patterns regardless of age, race or gender, [so] everyone can find a rhythm to help them combine work with their other responsibilities or aspirations' (www.dti.gov.uk/work – lifebalance/what.html). The Labour government commitment to WLB can be seen in its establishment of the Challenge Fund, in 2000, which provides funds for organizations to introduce new working arrangements to benefit the organization, its customers and employees. The key to WLB in employment terms is a range of flexible work arrangements framed in policies and procedures, such as part-time working, temporary working, jobsharing, home and teleworking, flexitime and flexible working hours, compressed working weeks, annualized hours, career breaks and outsourcing.

The term work – life balance includes a number of aspects as follows:

- how long people work (flexibility in the number of hours worked);
- when people work (flexibility in the arrangement of hours);
- where people work (flexibility in the place of work);
- developing people through training so that they can manage the balance better;
- providing back-up support; and
- breaks from work.

(Glynn et al. 2002: 9)

Though WLB constitutes 'complex phenomena of adjusting working life and family life' (Tyrkko 2002: 107), there is evidence that there is now a high level of support for work – life balance from both employers and employees (Hogarth et al. 2001). Further, 'discussion of work – life balance and family-friendly employment is much in vogue among politicians and business leaders' (Felstead et al. 2002: 54). Evidently the public sector on the whole is more committed to WLB than the private sector (Persaud 2001), although in addition to public sector organizations, service sector and large organizations have been found to have significantly more flexibility than other organizations (Mayne et al. 1996). This article investigates work – life balance developments in the UK public sector. It explores developments at different levels of influence – namely macro, organizational and individual – and assesses the extent to which links between them enables optimal progression of the WLB agenda in the UK public sector.

LEVELS OF INFLUENCE ON WLB

The key levels of influence on WLB developments can be identified at the macro or socio-economic level, the level of the organization and that of the individual. Inevitably there is some fusion between these levels though each can be considered in turn.

The macro level

At this level, a number of inter-related drivers have encouraged the emergence of WLB (Maxwell 2004). These include economic and political forces, gender at work, changing employee perceptions of work and effects of technology.

Economic and political forces

Flexible work can be traced to the 1980s when the Conservative government of the day initiated deregulation of the labour market in the UK in order to achieve greater efficiency and productivity in British industry as a whole (Dex and McCulloch 1997). The background to this was economic recession and a workforce, especially in the public sector, characterized by job demarcation, inflexibility and unionization. Thus the primary drivers of WLB were political and economic. Curson (1986) asserts that employment strategies in the early 1980s were shaped by three factors in organizations: first, a drive to achieve a permanent reduction in unit labour costs; second, a reluctance to increase the number of permanent, full-time staff; and third, a need to identify new patterns of working to limit unit labour costs.

By the late 1990s, different types of flexible working were evident across UK industry, more so in the public than private sector (Cully 1998). Further, the Labour government returned in 1997 took up the Conservatives' initiative on flexible working by including it in their manifesto. WLB was now recast in political terms, as more an individual right than an economic imperative.

According to the Industrial Relation Survey (IRS) *Employment Trends*, 'developments on the work – life balance issue [were] incessant during 2000' (1999: 12). A range of actions spurred the WLB debate at this time: the launch of the Government's work – life campaign and first Work – Life Balance Week; the establishment of the organization Employers for Work – Life Balance; and the introduction of family-friendly legislation. Since then, the momentum of interest has apparently been sustained and can be seen in the increasing amount of employment law, most notably the wide-ranging 2002 Employment Act. A key part of this piece of legislation is the employee right to request part-time working.

Gender at work

The increasing proportion of women in the labour market has, as Kirkton and Greene (2000) assert, been an important change in the social and economic fabric of the UK over the past few decades. Women now comprise 51 per cent of the workforce, according to the *Labour Force Survey* (2002) and have arguably influenced its characteristics. Bardoel *et al.* (1999), for example, hypothesize that working women generally may predispose organizations to offer more WLB practices due to their caring responsibilities for child and elderly dependants.

Indeed for some researchers gender is central to WLB as economically active females typically assume more family responsibilities than their male counterparts (Sullivan and Lewis 2001; Pillinger 2002). Consequently, mothers, especially those with children under the age of 13 years, tend to experience more conflict in achieving WLB than fathers (Higgins et al. 1994; Fu and Shafer 2001). Where working mothers see their primary role as a mother and their secondary role as an employee but spend more time than they would like at work there is likely to be heightened conflict (Carlson et al. 1995). Flexibility in working hours clearly has a role here. Also, 'the rising incidence of family breakdown in the UK has resulted in more employees having sole responsibility for children or complex arrangements involving ex-partners and stepchildren' (IRS Management Review 24, 2002: 2). Such is the impact of carer responsibilities, which usually but not always fall to women, that Coyne (2002: 447) has raised the question that care giving may have become 'the new class ceiling'. Moreover, dissatisfaction with either family or work roles can have a negative, cross-over effect on the other role domain for all parents (Williams and Alliger 1994). It has been found however that positive marital and parental roles can mitigate the effects of poor job experiences for women (Barnett 1994). Further, there is evidence that conflict between work and family roles is reduced when work and family roles reinforce similar values (Lobel 1992).

There is an argument therefore that the greater participation of women in work, combined with the growing complexity of families, encourages the development of WLB practices in organizations. Strachan and Burgess (1998) go beyond this contention in asserting that there can be a bias of WLB arrangements towards women. Similarly Bailyn (1992) contends that the UK focus of flexible working arrangements has been working mothers. Despite this it appears that there is not perception of inherent unfairness due to carer – and therefore gender – bias in WLB in the UK (Hogarth et al. 2001).

Changing employee perceptions of work

Arguably there is a changing societal perception about the value of work. Indeed, it has been argued that a new psychological contract exists for many employees in the modern world (Sims 1994). This contract frames what organizations and individuals expect to exchange in their employment relationship. Increasingly, the desire for WLB seems to be a feature of this exchange. For example Worrall and Cooper (1999) assert that public sector workers and junior managers place more value on their home than working lives. While Amos-Wilson (1993) suggests that, for women, career development is influenced by their attitudes on motherhood. In the same vein, Huldi's research (2002) strongly suggests that graduates with childcare responsibilities participate less in working life. Lastly, in Vincola's (1999) discussion of the Families and Work Institute (1997) national study of the changing UK workforce, the notion is raised that there is extending employee interest in a range of options from reducing work in their lives, to the extreme of giving up careers. Above all, perceptions of work, particularly with a WLB dimension, may be a function of age. Shabi (2002) makes the point that employment surveys in general apparently highlight a distinct attitude to work among Generation X (those born after 1963). This generation seeks a lifestyle that includes non-work time regardless of other responsibilities. They also have increased confidence in their employment skills and prospects, and less employer loyalty.

The effects of technology
The growth in sophistication and application of different types of technology has also been a driver in the expansion of 24 x 7 businesses and a long hours culture in recent years. Lester (2000) makes the point that technology can both help and hinder WLB, by making work more accessible at all times of the day and night, and also in enabling a more flexible approach to when and where work should be carried out. This reflects Glynn *et al.*'s (2002) point, made earlier, about the dimension of flexibility in the place of work.

The organizational level

Changing models of flexibility
Atkinson's model of the Flexible Firm, proposed in the mid-1980s, is arguably the most innovative and influential of the models of flexible work from the 1980s. Here the workforce is divided into two distinct groups: core and peripheral employees. The core employees are full-time, permanent staff. The peripheral employees constitute the flexible workforce in terms of numerical flexibility (their numbers can be expanded or contracted quickly), functional flexibility (their skills can be varied) and financial flexibility (their rates of pay can be varied). Notwithstanding the debate surrounding Atkinson's model (Proctor and Ackroyd 2001), the model itself acted to provide a bridge head to the possibilities of flexible work, including working time and place flexibility. The Chartered Institute of Personnel and Development reports that in the period 1985 to 2000 there was a 'large increase in flexible working both in response to market pressure and to meet employees' needs to balance work and family life' (2000: ix). Further, Osterman (1995) suggests that the adoption of WLB policies and practices often represents a response to employee requests for flexible work.

Benefits of work – life balance
Organizational benefits have been identified in terms of improved retention and recruitment positioning from WLB (CIPD 2000); easier service delivery (Hogarth *et al.* 2000), which is important in a market orientated culture that increasingly includes the

public sector (Armstrong and Baron 1998); enhanced quality service (Lasch 1999); decreased staff turnover (Management Services 2002) and absence (Glynn *et al.* 2002); enhanced employee capability (Tombari and Spinks 1999); and employee flexibility and skills to succeed in rapidly changing markets (Vincola 1999). Possibly, the more people-focused the organization, the greater the benefits from WLB, building on Baron and Collard's view that there is 'a positive relationship between more sophisticated/ innovative people management practices and improved organisational performance' (1999: 38). Moreover, the organizational benefits that may accrue from WLB may fuel the drivers that encourage organizations to consider WLB policies and practices.

Managers and WLB

The crux of translating WLB policies into practice is the managers – and supervisors – who make the operational decisions about WLB at work. These people can be seen as the critical agents in WLB. Tombari and Spinks (1999) identify from their research that management support is critical to WLB initiatives. Similarly Kropf (1999) comments that poor supervisor skills and behaviours can inhibit WLB in practice. Where there is resistance from managers on WLB, Watkins (1995) proposes ways of overcoming defensive reasoning on WLB, emphasizing the role of organizational culture in supporting WLB. Other writers have also commented on the significance of organizational culture in WLB (Gonyea and Googins 1992; Kramar 1997; Kropf 1999; Tombari and Spinks 1999; Shabi 2002). Glynn *et al.* highlight the significance of managers in this respect:

> ... whether an individual feels able to discuss issues outside of work, request different ways of working and believe that the organisation genuinely enables balance will depend considerably on the skills of the manager in creating an open communication culture of trust and respect.
>
> (2002: 8)

Managers' views on and inclinations towards WLB may be influenced by their typically working long hours themselves. This is the case particularly for men (Hogarth *et al.* 2001). Employee requests for flexibility may conceivably be seen by already stretched managers as an additional pressure (Glynn *et al.* 2002). Thus there may be a potential tension, even a disconnection, between employees and their managers in WLB. Glynn *et al.* suggest that 'for managers to enable work–life balance for themselves and others, a three-way relationship between the organization, the manager and the employee base must be obtained' (2002: 32).

The individual level

At the individual level, there are potentially important benefits from being better able to balance work commitments with other life elements. Such benefits include less role conflict for working mothers and carers (Carlson *et al.* 1995). Directly related to this is more quality time with dependants (Hogarth *et al.* 2001); maximization of employees' control over their lives (Sims 1994); and 'happier staff' (Hogarth *et al.* 2001: 371). In addition individuals report improved productivity, motivation and commitment as a result of improved WLB (CIPD 2000). Therefore, through employees finding an appropriate WLB, there is the potential for improvements in organizational performance. Again, it is worth noting that these benefits may generate more interest in WLB for organizations considering adopting such practices.

RESEARCH QUESTIONS

As can be seen there is a substantial track record of research on WLB issues at each of the three levels of influence of macro, organizational and individual. However connections between levels of influence have not been addressed to date (Gonas 2002). Yet in the current context of a 'Best Value' approach to public expenditure that is the model in UK public services, it could be argued that the link between such levels may be particularly relevant in ensuring optimization of resources. It was therefore decided to formulate a research aim of exploring the links between macro, organizational and individual levels of influence in WLB. The research aim was deconstructed into the following research questions: What are the drivers of WLB? What are the effects and implications of WLB policies and practices? What are the issues for line managers? What are the impacts of WLB arrangements for individuals who experience them?

RESEARCH DESIGN

Much of the empirical work on the topic of WLB adopts a phenomenological case study approach, as a traditional approach to qualitative inquiry (Creswell 1998). The empirical work reported here uses this approach to develop exploratory and explanatory case studies (Yin 2003). With the research aim of exploring current developments in WLB policies and practices in UK public management at macro, organizational and individual levels, the primary research, comprises seven case organizations.[1] These organizations are specified below, together with a brief descriptor.

(1)   *Central Scotland Forest Trust*: a publicly funded, small organization with charitable status; its mission is to 'lead and secure the creation of the Central Scotland Forest', an area of around 166 000 hectares within which approximately three-quarters of a million people live.

(2)   *Quarriers*: a long-established, very large voluntary agency that provides a range of service for children, families and people with disability; its mission is 'working

together to overcome personal and social disadvantage, inspire optimism, create opportunity and offer choice to children, families and others in need of support'.

(3)   *Scottish Court Service*: Scottish national court service comprising fifty-two court sites across agency headquarters, Supreme Courts and Sheriff Courts. Its purpose is to 'help secure ready access to justice for the people of Scotland, delivering a high quality service to all who use the courts'.

(4)   *Falkirk Council*: a public sector organization employing over 7,000 people to provide services such as education, housing and social work, community initiatives, development, finance, law and administration, corporate and commercial functions.

(5)   *Lauder College*: a further education institution aiming to offer high-quality, innovative and accessible learning and business services that contribute to quality of life, choice and prosperity for its customers and communities.

(6)   *Lothian and Borders Police Force*: with a police strength of around 2,600 and civilian staff of 1,100, the centre of policy development and operational goals is 'to prevent crime, keep the peace, protect and reassure the community, uphold the law firmly and fairly, and pursue and identify those who break the law'.

(7)   *HM Prison Barlinnie*: Scotland's largest prison, located in Glasgow, which aims to 'keep in custody those committed by the courts, maintain good order, care for prisoners with humanity, and provide prisoners with a range of opportunities to exercise personal responsibility and prepare for release'.

These case organizations were selected purposively (Stake 1995) on two criteria: they had WLB policies and procedures in place; individual employees had experienced an aspect of these policies and procedures. In order to encapsulate as many facets of WLB, the authors selected the particular WLB arrangements under investigation in each case. The methods of data capture in each organization were uniform: a series of semi-structured, in-depth interviews and documentary evidence. In each case, there were four informants to glean different organizational perspectives: a chief executive officer, or equivalent; a human resource specialist; an employee who has experienced a work–life balance arrangement and her/his line manager. The reason for this configuration was to achieve depth of analysis and to allow for the identification of connections at macro, organizational and individual levels (Gonas 2002), as discussed earlier. The individual employees were self-selected; their participation in the research snow-balled to include their line managers. The rich data yielded were reduced by using the principal questions as coding categories (Robson 2002), which subsequently allowed the compilation of 'inferential information' (Miles and Huberman 1994: 56).

  The main advantage of the research design is that it supports the overall research aim and specific empirical purpose in a way that allows for corroboration of findings. The series of interviews was seen as important, in Boje's terms, to seek an alternative 'to the fiat of the single-voiced, single-authoured narrative dictating organisation memory' (2001: 9). Moreover, as the personal issues giving rise to WLB can be sensitive, face-to-face interviews over an hour or so, were considered important in ethical terms. The 'social process' (Easterby-Smith *et al*. 2002: 131) of interviews was of heightened importance due to the potential sensitivity and personal nature of the research topic.

There are three main limitations in the research design. First, case studies by their very nature can lack generalizability. This limitation is underlined by the non-probability sampling technique used in each case. However, the findings are not claimed to be universal, rather they may be indicative of specific learning points associated with WLB. The second limitation is intrinsic in that in-depth interviews can yield substantial amounts of rich data from which it is challenging to identify converging lines of findings. Content analysis of the interviews on repeated views limited the impact of this disadvantage. The third limitation is extrinsic and lies in the possibility that the key findings may not translate to other case organizations. However, the principle that experiential learning is valuable offsets this limitation.

CASE STUDY FINDINGS

Forms of flexibility

The most frequently occurring forms of flexibility offered by the case study organizations are shown in Table 1. Others included: drugs/alcohol counselling (4), career breaks (3), special shift arrangements (3), carer leave (3), sick children leave (3), nursery/creche (3), public/community service (3), stress counselling (3), sports achievement leave (3), occupational health (3), annualized hours (2), home working (2), term-time working (2), voluntary reduced time (2), responsibility breaks (2), respite arrangements (2), confidential help (2), compressed hours (1), debt/financial advice (1).

Influences at a macro level

Macro, external-level influences, as a rationale for introducing WLB, were cited in several cases by respondents at chief executive level. For example, in the cases of the Central Scotland Forest Trust and Falkirk Council, applications had been made to the DTI Challenge Fund. The Government's emphasis on equality in public service (e.g. HM Prison Barlinnie) and the valuing people agenda (Scottish Court Service) were raised too. Also important were recent changes in employment law and tightening labour markets. These factors were acknowledged to have encouraged the development of organizational WLB policies.

Table 1: Most frequently occurring forms of flexibility offered by the case study organizations

Form of flexibility	No. of cases (N = 7)
Parental/paternity leave	7
Study leave	7
Flexitime	6
Part-time working	5
Job sharing	5
Emergency leave	5
Extra maternity leave	5

Organizational level

Drivers of WLB

Two themes in particular were consistent across all of the case studies on the organizational rationale for introducing WLB initiatives. The first of these was to improve the recruitment of the best people. In almost half of the cases, this was linked to the explicit desire to implement an equality/managing diversity policy, and to alter the profile of the workforce. These were organizations that historically had a particularly male employee population, e.g. the prison and police services, but where now it was important to attract 'more of a mixed range of people'. Some of the other organizations in the study had particular challenges in recruitment. Falkirk Council described having considerable competition from other public service organizations for the same pool of staff; while another (Central Scotland Forest Trust) highlighted the geographically isolated location of the organization, which made it potentially unattractive because of issues of travelling and transport costs. Here WLB was seen as providing an edge in being perceived as an attractive employer. The second common theme was to improve retention of staff. Exit interviews tended to suggest that 'the need to be more flexible and take into account their personal circumstances' was increasingly important to staff. The significance of recruitment and retention reflect points raised by Sims (1994), the CIPD (2000) and Hogarth et al. (2001). These two themes represent organizational issues that have helped to reinforce the need for WLB policies.

WLB as a manifestation of culture and values was also apparent in several cases, mirroring Watkins' (1995) position. Quarriers cited an additional part of their rationale for involvement in WLB as being related to the value set of the organization, which 'is about people being important and recognizing individuality . . . and this applies to staff as well as service users'. Lauder College identified that an emphasis on human resources was a core organizational value 'as everything is dependent on staff skills, expertise and commitment'. WLB was seen there as a means of maintaining staff wellbeing in a world that is increasingly demanding and stressful (Worrall and Cooper 1999; Hogarth *et al.* 2001).

Effects and implications of WLB policies and practices

All of the case study organizations indicated that there had been very positive effects from the WLB policies and practices. In over half of the cases, it was highlighted that the management of stress was greatly benefited by WLB initiatives. The Chief Executive of Lauder College identified that 'there has been a noticeable impact on stress . . . (resulting in) a more positive approach and higher quality performance'. An outcome of the effective management of stress was the improvement of levels of attendance at work, as noted by Glynn *et al.* (2002). Improved employee performance (Lasch 1999) was also cited as important in almost half of the cases. This was described as being the result of having more positive staff with higher morale, who have 'a feeling of being valued' and who can continue to contribute even though their personal circumstances changed. Another aspect of improved performance was the facility to widen the hours of service provision to clients because of the flexibility offered to staff (cf. Armstrong and Baron 1998). It was also said that cultural issues were linked to WLB initiatives, and this was described in various ways. Lauder College described this as generating a culture of honesty where staff can admit to home problems where they exist. In a second case (Central Scotland Forest Trust) this was described as putting a value on the outcomes rather than simply the pattern of work, which in turn helps to foster a culture of trust. For a third case – Falkirk Council – it was said that 'WLB signals the value of staff'. Other effects were an improved employee relations climate; and improved relations with external stakeholders including personal partners and potential job candidates.

As to organizational problems or issues, it was highlighted in a few cases that the consultation processes which were ideally involved in introducing WLB could make progress rather slow, as could the need to pilot or trial particular initiatives. There was also the potential problem of disrupting work because of flexibility, and the requirement to ensure appropriate job cover. Other issues related to a concern that employees' expectations would be raised in that they could rearrange their schedules with minimal concern for work outputs; and the 'disenfranchisement' of staff who did not take advantage of such policies.

It was suggested by respondents that there are important communication issues in WLB including the need to promote practices internally to current staff, as well as externally to potential employees. In addition it was important not to over-extend employees' expectations about what is possible, and so they need to know that there may be restrictions on WLB arrangements and that these will depend on the nature of the work. A key element was honesty in feedback to staff during the development of WLB arrangements; together with strategies to ensure that staff do not develop misunderstandings that they have additional types of leave – 'almost as holidays' – to use up.

Line manager issues

Many managers considered there were advantages to them in implementing WLB policies, echoing Vincola's (1999) assertion. A manager in HM Prison Barlinnie commented: 'it does make life easier as a manager that you can be flexible. When you ask for something, staff will give support'. The existence of WLB policies meant that there were options for helping staff, and made the management role less difficult. As a result, open discussions about work were possible, and staff were more helpful. Such policies reduced absenteeism, and this was also positive for line managers. Greater employee flexibility in attitude and tasks was also highlighted as an unexpected outcome of implementing WLB policies.

It was frequently raised that there were considerable practical implications of implementing WLB policies, particularly planning to ensure that operational needs were met, and that this could result in 'some inconvenience'. Challenges existed in the consistency – or often lack of it – between the implementation of WLB policies by different line managers. Sceptical managers could be problematic in providing discouragement to staff on WLB (Kropf 1999). One instance in Lauder College was highlighted where a manager in this category required to access policies because of his own personal situation, and thereafter was extremely encouraging and supportive of his staff. It was suggested that there was a need to review workloads in a holistic way, to ensure that all team members' needs were being addressed when WLB practices are being arranged. It was also suggested that it would be desirable for staff to think about the business cases for a change in working arrangements rather than singularly focusing on their personal perspective. Aligning expectations of WLB to their understanding of the business needs was likely to be an important element of taking forward a WLB agenda in a number of the case study organizations.

Across the board of the cases, it was considered that managing WLB requires strong leadership together with clear commitment from the top, and that WLB should be integrated into the overall strategic change agenda. Managers require a clear awareness that WLB is a part of their role rather than being located with specialist human resource employees. However, given the increasing demands on the line manager role it was suggested that training and coaching for line managers is a key element in helping them implement WLB policies and make good decisions. Clearly this is central to progressing WLB in practice in the public sector.

Individual level

Specific individuals who had accessed WLB policies considered themselves to be more motivated at work and loyal to the organization than they were previously. Furthermore they identified that they were keen to repay the benefits they had gained through their increased commitment and improved performance. Two individuals, in the Scottish Court Service and Lauder College, who had had carer leave in particularly difficult circumstances could not emphasize this enough. In addition, an employee in Falkirk Council highlighted that WLB would be something he would explore explicitly when seeking a new job, arguably reflecting changing perceptions of work (Shabi 2002). The theoretical positions on WLB allowing more quality time with dependants (Hogarth *et al.* 2001) and the maximization of employees' control over their lives (Sims 1994) are implicit in the individual employee perspectives. As a result, 'happier staff' (Hogarth *et al.* 2001: 371) feel they give more to their employer and, arguably, come to seek WLB policies from their employer.

DISCUSSION OF IMPLICATIONS FOR PRACTICE

It seems in the case studies that the emergence of WLB in the UK public sector has been encouraged by several macro-level factors. Political forces at government level have been particularly important, especially the equality and valuing people agendas that are of current significance, and financial incentive in the form of the DTI Challenge Fund. Changes in employment law promoting flexible work and in the labour market in terms of shortages in supply have also acted to support the development of WLB policies. The factors of governmental forces, financial incentive and changes in employment law reflect current theory on WLB. However this study finds the influence of labour market shortages too is an emerging influence of significance in WLB development in the UK public sector.

Nevertheless, the main drivers for the development of WLB policies and practices in the case organizations tended to be focused at the organizational level. This has often been in response or subsequent to some macro-level influences. At the level of the organization, WLB was introduced primarily as a means of delivering human resource agendas in improving recruitment and retention, and second as a means of manifesting and promoting a people-valuing culture. There was little evidence of measurement or evaluation of the achievement of these aspirations having taken place, though benefits of WLB were described by the senior and line manager organizational representatives in terms such as improvements in attendance, performance and employee relations, reflecting the literature. It could be argued that in the context of Best Value, a greater focus on assessing the impact of WLB policies would be appropriate and should be implemented in the UK public sector. Furthermore, there is an argument that government should consider making mandatory the evaluation of WLB policies in this sector.

At the organizational level there are also important implications for senior and first line managers. For the former, active support of WLB policies is key together with effective communication and employee consultation on the development and implementation of WLB practices. For the latter training and coaching in the implementation of WLB practices is crucial. This study strongly suggests that managers

— both senior and first line — provide an all-important bridge between policy and practice. This is a point not yet emphasized in other WLB research.

As to the individual level, there was limited evidence of individuals in organizations driving an agenda of WLB in this study, in contrast to the position of the literature on this point. This will possibly change through time as the employees working for organizations that are current leaders in WLB seek such practices when they chose to move employer. Many organizations were keen to emphasize the need for balance in employee expectations, so that work-related needs did not become overshadowed by individuals' desires to manage their work to suit themselves entirely. Mutuality in organizational and individual needs seems to be key to effective implementation of WLB policies. When WLB policies have been successfully implemented in the case study organizations, there is significant evidence of the employees who have experienced the policies bringing additional levels of performance to their jobs. Therefore it seems that there is another type of mutuality involved in WLB, namely organizational and individual benefits. Thus clear connections between organizational and individual levels in terms of mutuality in both needs and benefits are arguably necessary for the effective development and implementation of WLB in the UK public sector.

CONCLUSIONS

The empirical research undertaken for this article strongly suggests that the connections between macro, organizational and individual levels are critical in WLB policies and practices. Moreover, the effectiveness of WLB for employees and employers alike hinges on the immediate line managers of individual employees taking up WLB arrangements. Theoretical perspectives on WLB thus far do not recognize these points. However, given the case study approach and non-probability sampling selection of research informants within the cases, further research on the connections between levels of influence in the UK is needed to substantiate these assertions. Another, related direction of further research signalled by the case research covered here is the impact of WLB practices on employees who are not taking up these arrangements.

The continuing and extending interest in WLB necessitates further research in order to extend insights into both the theory and practice of WLB. That the case work in this article corroborates much of the existing theory but exposes new aspects of WLB underlines this contention. The newly exposed dimensions of WLB include: managing consultation processes and piloting WLB initiatives that are time-consuming; managing employee expectations of WLB and framing them within the business needs; ensuring effective communication of WLB arrangements; and incorporating WLB in strategic change agendas that are a current preoccupation in many public sector organizations.

Addressing such challenges may be the way to develop further and sustain WLB in the UK public sector.

NOTE

1   Material from these case studies by the authors features in the book *Take the Time* (2003), published as a joint Equality Exchange, Fair Play Scotland and Department of Trade and Industry initiative.

REFERENCES

Amos-Wilson, P. (1993) 'Accomplishing Carer Development Tasks: Are There Gender Related Differences?'. *International Journal of Career Management*, 5:5 pp11 – 19.

Armstrong, M. and Baron, A. (1998) *Performance Management*, London: Institute of Personnel Management.

Bailyn, L. (1992) 'Issues of Work and Family in Different National Contexts: How the US, UK and Sweden Respond'. *Human Resource Management*, 31:8 pp201 – 9.

Bardoel, E. A., Moss, S. A., Smyrnois, K. and Tharenou, P. (1999) 'Employee Characteristics Associated with the Provision of Work Family Policy and Programs'. *International Journal of Manpower*, 20:8 pp563 – 77.

Barnett, R. C. (1994) 'Home to Work Spillover Revisited: A Study of Full Time Employed Women in Dual Earner Couples'. *Journal of Marriage and the Family*, 56:3 pp647 – 56.

Baron, A. and Collard, R. (1998) 'Realising Our Assets'. *People Management*, 5:20 pp38 – 45.

Boje, D. M. (2001) *Narrative Methods for Organisational and Communication Research*. London: Sage Publications.

Carlson, D. S., Kacmar, K. M. and Stepins, L. P. (1995) 'An Examination of Two Aspects of Work – Family Conflict; Time and Identity'. *Women in Management Review*, 10:2 pp17 – 25.

Chartered Institute of Personnel and Development (CIPD) (2000) 'Getting the Right Work – life Balance'. Research Report, October.

Coyne, B. S. (2002) 'Has Care Giving Become the New Class Ceiling? A Cross-Cultural Comparison of UK/US Responses by Lone Parents with Sole Care-Giving Responsibilities'. *Human Resource Development International*, 5:4 pp447 – 66.

Creswell, J. W. (1998) *Qualitative Inquiry and Research Design: Choosing among Five Traditions*, London: Sage Publications.

Cully, M. (1998) 'Workplace Employee Relations Survey: The World's Biggest Study Yet Carried Out into Employee Relations'. *People Management*, 29: October pp68 – 76.

Curson, C. (1986) *Flexible Patterns of Work*, London: Institute of Personnel Management.

Dex, S. and McCulloch, A. (1997) *Flexible Employment: the Future of Britain's Jobs*, London: MacMillan Press.

Easterby-Smith, M., Thorpe, R. and Lowe, A. (2002) *Management Research: An Introduction* (2nd edn), London: Sage Publications.

Felstead, A., Jewson, N., Phizacklea, A. and Walters, S. (2002) 'Opportunities to Work at Home in the Context of Work – Life Balance'. *Human Resource Management Journal*, 12:1 pp54 – 76.

Fu, C. K. and Shafer, M. A. (2001) 'The Tug of Work and Family'. *Personnel Review*, 30:5 pp502 – 22.

Glynn, C., Steinberg, I. and McCartney, C. (2002) 'Work – Life Balance: The Role of the Manager', West Sussex: Roffey Park Institute.

Gonas, L. (2002) 'Balancing Family and Work – to Create a New Social Order'. *Economic and Industrial Democracy*, 23:1 pp59 – 66.

Gonyea, J. G. and Googins, B. K. (1992) 'Linking the Worlds of Work and Family: Beyond the Productivity Trap'. *Human Resource Management*, 31:3 pp209 – 26.

Higgins, C., Duxbury, L. and Lee, C. (1994) 'Impact of Life Cycle Stage and Gender on the Ability to Balance Work and Family Responsibilities'. *Family Relations*, 43:2 pp144 – 50.

Hogarth, T., Hasluck, C. and Pierre, G. (2001) 'Work – Life Balance 2000: Results from the Baseline Study'. *Labour Market Trends*, 109:7 pp371 – 3.

Huldi, C. S. (2002) 'Family Obligations and the Transition to Working Life: The Influence of Parenthood and Family Obligations on the Transition to Employment of University Graduates'. *Education and Training*, 44:4/5 pp208 – 16.

Industrial Relations Service (IRS) Employment Trends (1999) Nos 693 and 704.

Industrial Relations Service (IRS) Management Review (2002) 'Work/Life Balance'. Issue 24.

Kirkton, G. and Greene, A. M. (2000) *The Dynamics of Managing Diversity: A Critical Approach*, Oxford: Butterworth Heineman.

Kramar, R. (1997) 'Developing and Implementing Work and Family Policies: The Implications for Human Resource Policies'. *Asia Pacific Journal of Human Resources* (Australia), 35:3 pp1 – 19.

Kropf, M. B. (1999) 'Flexibility Initiatives: Current Approaches and Effective Strategies'. *Women in Management Review*, 14:5 pp177 – 86.

Labour Force Survey (2002) Nomis, November. Available at http://parus.dur.ac.uk/.

Lasch, E. (1999) 'Achieving a Balance'. *Ohio Certified Public Accounts Journal*, 58:1 pp21 – 2.

Lester, S. (1999) 'Technology's Effect on Work – Life Balance'. *Journal of European Industrial Training*, 23:7 p141.

Lobel, S. A. (1992) 'A Value Laden Approach to Integrating Work and Family Life'. *Human Resource Management*, 31:3 pp249 – 66.

Management Services (2002) 'Workplace Culture Fails to Support Work – Life Balance'. June.

Maxwell, G. (2004) 'Checks and Balances: The Role of Managers in Work – Life Balance'. *Journal of Retailing and Consumer Services*, forthcoming.

Mayne, L., Tregaskis, O. and Brewster, C. (1996) 'A Comparative Analysis of the Link between Flexibility and HRM Strategy'. *Employee Relations*, 18:3 pp5 – 24.

Miles, M. B. and Huberman, A. M. (1994) *Qualitative Data Analysis: An Expanded Sourcebook* (2nd edn), London: Sage Publications.

Osterman, P. (1995) 'Work/Family Programs and the Employment Relationship'. *Administrative Science Quarterly*, 40:4 p681 – 700.

Persaud, J. (2001) 'Does the Private Sector Believe That Work – Life Balance Is for Wimps?'. *Human Resources*, September pp38, 40 – 3, 45.

Pillinger, J. (2002) 'The Politics of Time: Can Work – Life Balance Really Work?'. *Equal Opportunities Review*, 107:July pp18 – 21.

Proctor, S. and Ackroyd, S. (2001) 'Flexibility' chapter 8 in T. Redman and A. Wilinson (eds) *Contemporary Human Resource Management: Text and Cases*. Essex, UK: Financial Times and Prentice Hall.

Robson, C. (2002) *Real World Research* (2nd edn), London: Sage Publications.

Shabi, R. (2002) 'Flex Appeal'. *Management Accounting*, 78:6 pp20 – 1.

Sims, R. R. (1994) 'Human Resource Management's Role in Clarifying the New Psychological Contract'. *Human Resource Management*, 33:3 pp373 – 83.

Strachan, G. and Burgess, J. (1998) 'The Family Friendly Workplace'. *International Journal of Manpower*, 19:4 pp250 – 65.

Stake, R. (1995) *The Art of Case Study Research*, London: Sage Publications.

Sullivan, C. and Lewis, S. (2001) 'Home-Based Telework, Gender and the Syncronisation of Work and Family: Perspectives of Teleworkers and Their Co-residents'. *Gender, Work and Organization*, 18:2 pp123 – 45.

Tombari, N. and Spinks, N. (1999) 'The Work – Family Interface at the Royal Bank Financial Group: Successful Solutions – a Retrospective Look at Lessons Learned'. *Women in Management Review*, 14:5 pp186 – 94.

Tyrkko, A. (2002) 'The Intersection between Working Life and Parenthood: A Literature Review'. *Economic and Industrial Democracy*, 23:1 pp107 – 23.

Vincola, A. (1999) 'Good Career/Life Balance Makes for Better Workers'. *Human Resource Focus*, 76:4 p13.

Watkins, K. E. (1995) 'Changing Managers' Defensive Reasoning about Work – Family Conflicts'. *Journal of Management Development*, 14:2 pp77–88.

Williams, K. and Alliger, G. M. (1994) 'Role Stressors, Mood Spillover and Perceptions of Work – Family Conflict in Employed Parents'. *Academy of Management Journal*, 37:4 pp837–68.

Worrall, L. and Cooper, C. (1999) 'Working Patterns and Working Hours: Their Impact on UK Managers'. *Leadership and Organisation Development Journal*, 20:1 pp6–10. Available at www.dti.gov.uk/work–lifebalance/what.html.

Yin, R. K. (2003) *Applications of Case Study Research* (2nd edn), London: Sage Publications.

THE NEW PUBLIC MANAGEMENT AND THE UK POLICE SERVICE

The role of the police sergeant in the implementation of performance management

Reginald Butterfield, Christine Edwards and Jean Woodwall

INTRODUCTION

This article explores the implementation of individual performance management within the UK Police Service, following the introduction of the New Public Management (NPM) in the 1990s. Performance management systems are a key feature of the New Public Management. Their introduction within a UK City Police Service is examined at the level of the police sergeant who has a primary responsibility for managing the performance of individual police constables, and hence the service delivery within one of the UK's 'essential' public services. This is the first study to examine in detail the impact of NPM at the operational level in the Police Service. The article starts with a discussion of the concept of NPM and its impact on other public services. It then moves on to a consideration of the current debates around performance management within the New Public Management context. Information on the contextual developments within a large UK police authority, 'City Police Service', is followed by a discussion of the method of investigation and findings. Finally the article attempts to identify some of the implications for the implementation of performance management within organizations, and for New Public Management practice.

THE NEW PUBLIC MANAGEMENT

There is some difference of opinion about when the New Public Management first appeared in the UK. It can be traced back to the introduction of broadly similar administrative doctrines in public administration within OECD countries after 1979 (Hood 1991), but is more usually held to denote a second wave of reforms in the 1990s that has promoted management, consumerism and competition alongside the previous concern with efficiency (Pollitt 1993; Rhodes 1994; Hoggett 1996). None the less, there is some consensus that it involves a number of interconnected elements (Tonge and Horton 1996. These include the extensive use of competitive market and quasi-market mechanisms (Ferlie 1992; Mark and Scott 1992), privatization of public utilities, organizational restructuring including decentralization of management (but with simultaneous greater central control by means of performance-based funding); new styles of governance and organizational culture change (Ferlie 1992; Harrow and Shaw 1992; Ferlie and Pettigrew 1996). The latter includes a rhetoric of quality and focus upon the consumer, and, finally, a heavy emphasis upon organizational performance rather than procedures. This has involved the adoption of: 'a range of techniques including performance review, staff appraisal systems, performance related pay, scrutinies, so-called "quality audits", customer feedback mechanisms, comparative tables of performance indicators, chartermarks, customer charters, quality standards and TQM' (Hoggett 1996: 20).

The appropriateness of such techniques for the public sector has provoked intense debate, with a substantial body of opinion arguing that public sector organizations are very different from those in the private sector, and that NPM precepts are therefore inappropriate. It has been argued that the differences in organizational goals, environments, structures and managerial values mean that it is impossible to implement such managerial techniques successfully within the public sector (Ackroyd *et al.* 1989), and that the pattern of change is complex (Poole *et al.* 2002). While there are some signs of convergence, there are also significant differences in managerial attitudes, behaviour and experiences. However, the counter argument that there is little evidence of sharp differences between the public and private sector has recently been upheld by other research (Boyne 2002; Poole *et al.* 2002). None the less, the manner in which the techniques of NPM are implemented presents a major research problem.

THE PLACE OF PERFORMANCE MANAGEMENT WITHIN THE NEW PUBLIC MANAGEMENT

Performance management is a key element in the repertoire of NPM techniques drawn from Human Resource Management (HRM) and management accounting. In particular, the broad definition of the performance management model developed by the UK Audit Commission (1995) is based upon the integration of a number of management activities and functions. These include: defining and setting organizational and individual aims and objectives; corporate planning; linking organizational strategy and service objectives to jobs and clients; identifying staff training and development needs; assessing the results through personal appraisal using relevant performance indicators, performance agreements or contracts; using the knowledge gained through training to modify performance attitudes; external and internal communication systems; and organization development and performance review. Yet the place of performance management within the New Public Management has engendered a great deal of scholarly and professional debate. Much of this has been driven from the management accounting rather than the HRM perspective, and the introduction of the techniques used can be traced to the application of the principles of financial audit to the public sector (Power 1997; Nutley 2000), and particularly their promotion by the UK National Audit Office and the Audit Commission after the late 1980s. The three familiar criteria of economy, efficiency and effectiveness were combined within the concept of 'value for money' to create a mechanism for auditable performance measurement. Performance indicators became the tool for in-year monitoring and relating plans to outcomes, justifying the use of resources and assessing overall efficiency. The emphasis is upon the link between strategic plans and performance measures (Flynn 1997; Horton and Farnham 1999). However, there has been much criticism and in particular, Mohrman and Mohrman (1995) have criticized performance management systems for being too focused upon the individual employee, their manager and past performance. Also, the auditing of *outcomes* tends to be displaced by easily measurable *outputs*, and Smith (1995) has argued that it is still impossible to measure intangible outcomes. None the less, the search for solutions to this problem continues with complex systems models becoming increasingly popular (Carter *et al.* 1995; Rouse 1999; Boland and Fowler 2000).

But are such systems approaches to performance management adequate? As Power (1997) argues, these formalized control systems have more to do with sustaining a myth of control, and external legitimization than with any real improvements in operational efficiency. Holloway *et al.* (1999) illustrate this in their study of complex approaches to performance improvement within the UK National Health Service. They conclude that complex approaches are only as good as the people who apply them and the context in which they are applied. The competing demands of different elements of complex performance management systems can place pressure on employees to pursue the line of least resistance.

However, from the perspective of HRM, individual ability, motivation and opportunity tend to be the main concerns in performance management (Boxall and Purcell 2003; Purcell *et al.* 2003). While inevitably this has implications for a wide range of HRM processes (such as recruitment, selection, training and career development) pay and performance appraisal systems are the aspects of performance management that receive most attention – particularly in relation to professional and managerial groups. Armstrong and Barron (1998) argue that there are a wider range of factors that need to be taken into account when managing, measuring, modifying and rewarding individual performance: personal factors, management leadership, support from work teams, the nature of the work system and technologies and contextual factors relating to the internal and external environment. Contextual factors are particularly significant, indicating that individual opportunity is at least as important as individual ability and motivation. This makes the role of line managers critical, as has been demonstrated in recent research:

> Implementing and enacting policies is the task of line managers. The way they exercise leadership in the sense of communicating, solving problems, listening to suggestions, asking people's opinions, coaching and guiding and controlling lateness, absence and quality, makes the vital difference.
>
> (Purcell *et al.* 2003: 72)

They require easy access to valid and reliable information about their direct reports, adequate time to review performance at regular intervals, and to plan and take follow-up action, including the provision of training and development opportunities for staff. They also need to be trained in how to review performance. However recent research has shown that line managers are the weak link in the implementation of individual performance appraisal systems due to lack of incentives, inadequate training, a short-term focus and increasing pressure on time (Stiles *et al.* 1997; Harris 2001; Truss 2001). Thus, in the context of this article, the question therefore arises as to whether police sergeants were able to carry out their role effectively in individual performance appraisal, in the manner envisaged by the architects of New Public Management.

NEW PUBLIC MANAGEMENT, PERFORMANCE MANAGEMENT AND THE POLICE SERVICE

The impact of the changes brought about by the New Public Management arrived considerably later in the Police Service than in other parts of the UK public sector. The 'birth' of the NPM within the UK Police Service has been a slow and laborious process beset by political struggles made all the more difficult by the involvement of police authorities and government officials in the formation of policy for criminal law enforcement. The former UK Conservative government relied heavily upon the police to maintain public order during a number of industrial relations disputes. This meant that the police were not substantially affected by NPM in the same way as other public services such as education and health, until the early 1990s. There had been some introduction of NPM practices during the 1980s such as: 'policing by objectives'; management planning with funding linked to performance; the introduction of performance management systems drawing largely upon input measures and the construction of a comprehensive set of national performance indicators. Also, during the 1990s, a customer-focused culture change programme known as the 'PLUS' programme that emphasized service to the public; 'sector policing' (a form of community policing); and diversity management policies were introduced. Much of this was largely influenced by the Audit Commission (Savage and Leishman 1996), and was taken up voluntarily by the Police Service, but little happened until a number of major government initiatives. These included the Sheehy Inquiry into the leadership pay and conditions of the police (HMSO 1993a), a White Paper on the structure and funding of police authorities (HMSO 1993b) and the Posen Inquiry into the delivery of services provided by the police (Cope *et al.* 1997). These proposals brought considerable resistance from both the Association of Chief Police Officers as well as the Police Federation (Butterfield 2001: 59–64).

The Police Service is one area of the public sector where the introduction of the NPM poses most dilemmas. While operating within a hierarchical structure, policing involves wide discretion at lower levels, most responses need to be reactive rather than strategic and there are considerable differences in intra-rank cultures (Savage and Leishman 1996). Police work involves long hours of work, and a degree of risk and social isolation from the public at large. These circumstances have generated a strong incestuous culture that has been identified as a major impediment to change. Despite some variation between departments, Peck (1994) describes the main characteristics of this culture as politically right of centre, a conservative/reactionary outlook, action oriented, authoritarian, judgemental, intolerant of 'wet' authority and conformist. Sergeants, moreover, are at the centre of this 'canteen' culture:

> The problem . . . is that these men [the more experienced ones on the relief] are the ones with nine or ten years of experience. They are the ones who set the tone in the canteen and in the van, as sergeants and inspectors they are part of the canteen culture themselves.
>
> (Graef 1989: X1)

A significant aspect of this culture was an 'us-and-them' mentality, not only between police and public but within the service itself, the main divide being between 'management cops' and 'street cops' (Reiner 1985). The extent to which the sergeant had been able to break out of this culture and identify more closely with management was, therefore, a question of some significance for this research when centrally set targets and performance indicators have to be adopted by sergeants and 'enforced' upon constables. From being 'one of the boys', police sergeants have had to distance themselves from their team when managing individual performance.

NEW PUBLIC MANAGEMENT WITHIN CITY POLICE SERVICE

The major changes to the structure and operating systems of 'City Police Service' were introduced in 1995 after the Sheehy Inquiry reported its findings. The result was a degree of delayering, decentralization and devolution of some operational responsibilities, notably those relating to Human Resource Management. The organization went from eight police operational units, known as 'areas' to five. The hierarchical layers of management went from ten to eight, as the posts of Chief Superintendent and Deputy Assistant Commissioner were removed, and that of Commander went 'off-line'. This high degree of control and accountability was achieved predominantly through the use of performance management techniques revolving around five Key Objectives, five Key Performance Indicators and thirty Police Service Performance Indicators covering call management, crime management, traffic management, public order management, community policing and resource/cost management (Butterfield 2001: 70 – 1). These were not drawn up by local police Commanders, but were set centrally by the Audit Commission, Her Majesty's Inspector of Constabulary and the Association of Chief Police Officers. At the individual level this was underpinned by a new performance appraisal system requiring all police officers up to the level of superintendent, to undergo a six-monthly performance interview followed by an objective setting interview at which both work-related objectives (driven by the divisional performance indicators) and personal objectives and training would be agreed.

What these changes meant for the role of the police sergeant was unclear. Historically, the role of supervising ranks was left to local forces to determine, as there had never been a national job definition for the police sergeant. In the case of City Police Service where there had been clearly defined job descriptions for all ranks from sergeant to chief inspector, they ceased to be produced in 1994, just before the NPM reforms. None the less, there were two typical roles undertaken by police sergeants at the time that the fieldwork was undertaken in the late 1990s. The first was the *relief/core sergeant* who had three aspects to his/her role: custody officer (the processing and welfare of prisoners), controller (the management of the local divisional control room and associated resources) and sector patrolling sergeant responsible for the supervision of street activity on a round-the-clock shift system. In contrast the *sector sergeant* was responsible for a small team of community orientated constables on a twenty-four-hour basis, and was expected to stand in for the relief/core sergeant if required because of sickness absence, annual leave or other public order duties. All sergeants reported into their immediate manager, the inspector, and there was typically one inspector per relief/core team and per sector team. Essentially the sergeant's role was predominantly that of an operational police officer with some supervisory responsibility. Sergeants were promoted from within the ranks and very much part of a close-knit team delivering services at the local level. They had a primary responsibility for the performance management of their constables, including appraisal, mentoring and training, welfare, discipline and team leadership.

The introduction of NPM within the Police Service in general and City Police Service in particular, raised the issue of whether the implementation of individual performance management would take place in a straightforward manner. In order to explore this issue the study attempted to answer a number of questions:

- To what extent did police sergeants have adequate time relative to their other responsibilities to carry out performance management of their constables, especially appraisal?
- Did the sergeants have access to valid and reliable information in order to conduct effective appraisal of their constables?
- To what extent were police sergeants able to provide follow-up support to their constables?
- To what extent did the performance appraisal process provide a means of integrating organizational strategy and service objectives with the work of individual police officers?

RESEARCH DESIGN

This research was conducted as part of a larger project examining the changing role of sergeants within the Police Service (Butterfield 2001) from the perspective of sergeants, constables, inspectors and senior management. As an employee of the Police Service up until his retirement in 1997, the principal researcher had extremely privileged access to data. Towards the end of his career he had assumed the role of a senior internal consultant which brought him into contact with the senior management of the Police Service, and thus access to considerable support for his research. This allowed the opportunity for data collection by means of interviews, limited observation and examination of records.

An interpretative research design was chosen because the primary research problem focused upon the implementation of performance management at the level of the sergeant, and because there were several stakeholders in this process. The first stage involved fifty semi-structured interviews and six focus groups drawing participants from three police divisions located at the centre, middle and periphery of the 'City Police Service' area. These were opportunity samples of participants attending training programmes delivered in the three divisions. The participants included senior managers, inspectors, sergeants and constables who had all been in post prior to the changes introduced after 1995.

The second stage of data collection was undertaken at two separate locations within the City Police Service, selected on the basis that they offered two entirely different types of policing environment and management styles, typical of the range within the City Police Service. Two role sets were studied at each location: one for relief/core sergeants, and one for sector sergeants. Each role set consisted of eight members (focal sergeant, peer sergeants, constables and inspectors) plus up to five members of the divisional management team. In seeking to understand the response of the sergeant to the implementation of performance management within the City Police Service, the research went beyond the sergeant's perceptions of these changes, to explore the perspectives of those actors surrounding the sergeant. Thus the research design centred upon role set analysis (Merton 1957; Katz and Kahn 1978), which is particularly helpful in indicating ways of measuring the outcomes of role performance in relation to expectations. Role expectations are formulated in a dynamic social context with a strong emphasis upon interaction, communication and expectation (Machin 1981; Tsui 1984a, 1984b; Fondas and Stewart 1994; Conway and Willcocks 1997). This approach is relevant to the research because it provides a contextually focused approach to examining how performance management is implemented at the level of the police sergeant. Data were collected by semi-structured interview (an innovative approach as role set analysis is usually carried out using standardized questionnaire instruments) informed by the findings of the first stage. The interviews covered a wide range of issues relating to how role set members perceived the sergeants enacted their role. The questions that were of relevance to this research focused upon perceived changes in work role activity, the operation of the performance appraisal system (including the setting of performance objectives, their impact upon work activity, development opportunities, the time taken up by this) and the link with the wider performance management system including the centrally set performance indicators. Interview data were supported by observations recorded in a reflective journal and a review of police records at both divisions. The 'siege mentality' culture of the police, which has been frequently commented upon, meant that it was not possible to tape record the interviews, but notes taken during the interview were immediately written up afterwards and subsequently entered into a spreadsheet for analysis. The framework for analysis drew upon the key subject areas identified at Stage I and data were compared between different respondents in the role sets and between the two study sites. Analytical memos were used as a means to make sense of the data analysis, which was conducted according to the principles of the constant comparative method (Strauss and Corbin 1998).

FINDINGS

It is not possible to report on all the findings within the scope of this article. However, the general findings in relation to each of the research questions are outlined below. The very rich interview data cannot be reported on in detail, but selected quotations are provided to illustrate the main themes that emerged.

CHANGES IN SERGEANTS' WORKLOADS AND THE TIME AVAILABLE FOR PERFORMANCE APPRAISAL

A key assumption of performance management systems is that all parties have sufficient time to conduct appraisals. The interviews and focus groups during Stage I indicated that sergeants had experienced a number of major changes in their job responsibilities and workloads since 1995. There had been a significant increase in the volume of tasks they were expected to carry out, and the overall nature of those tasks had changed giving their role a more managerial slant. In essence, the sergeant had moved from a predominantly operational police officer with a supervisory responsibility, to a first line manager who was less involved in operational police duty. This was illustrated in a number of major shifts of emphasis in responsibilities. Sergeants now had new managerial responsibility for crime supervision and budgets as well as increased responsibility for the planning of work and the deployment of teams, for financial management, for formal debriefing of constables after all projects or incidents and for handling complaints against the police made by the public. In particular, they had acquired increased responsibility for the management and supervision of crime investigation through the CRIS computer system, and the management of custody and detention through the CAD system (if they were relief sergeants).

The introduction of the New Public Management within the Police Service has been accompanied by considerable innovation in information communication technology to facilitate record keeping and monitoring of performance, and, ostensibly, to achieve greater efficiency. However, the computer systems that were introduced did not reduce the need for paperwork, and in many cases (such as the custody computer –

CAD) required duplication of effort, or else generated the demand for more effort (as in the case of the CRIS computer system). In all cases it meant a greater supervisory responsibility for the sergeants, while their individual performance became more visible and open to scrutiny. In the past, crime supervision had been predominantly a role for the CID under the supervision of the detective chief inspector. The introduction of the CRIS system transformed the sergeant into a crime manager responsible for the day-to-day supervision of all but the most serious or complex crimes, with uniform constables undertaking a greater investigative role.

> The crime desk used to check the crime reports and now I have to do it. I have to extract statistics from the computers so I can do the PCs' [police constables] appraisal and so it goes on. The performance indicators built into the computers mean that I can't let them slip for a few days like I could with the old file system.
>
> (Sector Sergeant 3 – Site 2)

> CRIS means we now supervise crime investigation ... The extra paperwork and constant supervision of CRIS, CAD, CRIMINT and so on. We just cannot take any more work.
>
> (Sector Sergeant 1 – Site 2)

As indicated, this tended to be accompanied by a considerable increase in paperwork, leaving little time to patrol the streets and support their constables. Responsibility for the conduct of individual annual performance appraisals of constables, the setting, allocation and monitoring of performance criteria for the team and follow-up development for constables was all required in addition to the extra duties outlined above.

This appeared to be a general trend. There was remarkable consensus about these developments among members of all four role sets and between the two sites. Their views on the sergeants' job content revealed that few tasks had been lost and several new ones had been inherited from the inspector (especially planning, financial management and greater involvement in serious incidents). Senior management and inspectors also recognized the difficulties that this presented for sergeants:

> They now have more responsibility and take on many of the things inspectors used to do. They have to be proactive and identify work for the team ... Crime supervision is totally new to them and the supervision is mainly through the CRIS. They have budgetary responsibility and have to plan things within the budgets.
>
> (Inspector 2 – Site 1)

> The performance indicators dictate what they do, and their colleagues affect how they go about it ... I influence them through the performance indicators, mainly.
>
> (Inspector 1 – Site 1)

Yes, changed a lot. They now have clear individual responsibility for specific things. They are also now problem-solvers instead of the inspectors. [They have] taken on more decision making. Case disposal is now more them.

(Senior Management Team Member 3 – Site 1)

They have to manage their budgets and keep up the performance indicators. Most of this wasn't around a few years ago and it is hard for them to fit it all in.

(Senior Management Team Member 2 – Site 2)

The sergeants who were interviewed all felt the increasing demands of greater responsibility for planning, supervision and communication with public 'customers'. The impact on their workload was significant.

I've changed a lot. I get more problems to deal with ... it also means I have to plan further ahead to get it all done.

(Sector Sergeant 3 – Site 2)

Weeks and months in advance depending on what I am looking at. Whereas before it was hours and sometimes days. The supervision aspect has grown considerably because of CRIS and other systems. I'm much more involved in planning and setting up projects.

(Relief Sergeant 2 – Site 1)

Take the CRIS system. When we had paper crime reports I just checked the initial entries and made sure all the relevant bits were filled in. The crime desk staff used to monitor the investigation and follow-up work ... Now I am responsible for the supervision of the whole exercise. I've never received training on how to do it, but I've got the job.

(Core Sergeant 2 – Site 2)

I also have to deal with the initial complaints from the public and go to community meetings. The main thing is to keep everybody happy and deliver the figures when it all boils down.

(Sector Sergeant 2 – Site 1)

The increasing demands of their role have led sergeants to exhibit the classic symptoms of role conflict. They had acquired new tasks without relinquishing the old ones, and this was particularly evident in terms of the expectations of their constables:

... it all just gets piled up on us. Nothing gets taken away. I don't go out with probationers any more and I have to rely on the more senior PCs to help them. That shouldn't be the case.

(Relief Sergeant 4 – Site 1)

Used to patrol and be in charge of policing, but not now ... PCs now do what they [sergeants] used to do. It was more disciplined in the past, and you knew what was expected. Sergeants no longer supervise or train PCs. The more senior PCs now do all of this, and the sergeants see less of us ... We get much less guidance now than in the past.

(Sector Constable 1 – Site 2)

The implication of this was that police sergeants were being expected to take a key role in a new and demanding performance appraisal process when they were also expected to take on additional responsibilities. Furthermore, these new responsibilities brought about a fundamental change in their work role that cut them off from the constables for whom they had responsibility. This affected both relief and sector sergeants. All these factors raise serious doubts as to whether sergeants had sufficient time to conduct appraisal of their constables in the prescribed manner.

ACCESS TO VALID AND RELIABLE INFORMATION TO ASSESS PERFORMANCE

A basic assumption underpinning all performance appraisal systems is that assessment of individual performance is based upon valid and reliable information. It has already been established that the changing work role of sergeants took them away from day-to-day contact with their constables. Additional responsibilities for managing computer information systems and other associated paperwork, but also the deployment of constables across a wide sector and on a twenty-four-hour basis, made regular contact difficult. This had two consequences in terms of collecting evidence for appraisals. It meant, on the one hand, that sergeants relied heavily on data generated from the computer systems, but on the other hand on their constables to provide further information. In the first case, constables often felt that only what was measured counted, and in the second case, sergeants and their inspectors expressed concern about the reliability of the evidence provided by the constables.

The PCs keep their own figures and we combine these with the computer ones. I mainly rely on the PCs as I don't have time to check things thoroughly. It's an exercise after all, so why worry about accuracy?

(Relief Sergeant 1 – Site 1)

Just an exercise really. It should be done better, but my inspector is always rushing about. We have a short chat and he writes up the performance bit. We never discuss figures because we both know that I am inside most of the time and he can get the custody numbers himself off the computer. It takes a lot of effort for no return. A waste of time. They don't even use the information for the promotion, so why do it?

(Core Sergeant 2 – Site 2)

... they get the reports back to check, but not the things that can't be measured. That's why I don't agree with the measurements. If I am witness to something or give my 'bodies' to a probationer, then none of this is shown, nor is the work we do on public order and this counts for a lot in [the city centre] ... They only measure the easy bits.

(Relief Constable 2 – Site 1)

... one of the problems is that the sergeants are relying too much on the PCs' help to complete the forms and this goes against what it is all about. They should be collecting evidence and not just figures – but they are not.

(Inspector 1 – Site 2)

The sergeants are supposed to discuss the performance and show the constables the evidence for specific points that they raise. Most sergeants rely on the PCs for the figures that aren't on the computer and even then the computer stats are often challenged as being wrong. Eventually they agree and write the report accordingly. It takes them a long time and they are always complaining about it.

(Inspector 2 – Site 2)

This meant that evaluations of performance were based upon selective use of *outputs* as recorded on the computer systems, or on the basis of anecdotal reports from constables, rather than demonstrated *outcomes* in terms of the service delivered. Questions therefore arose around the validity of such assessments. Second, with sergeants increasingly reliant upon information provided by constables with whom they were less frequently in contact, the reliability of their judgements in the appraisal process was also questionable.

SERGEANTS AND THE PROVISION OF FOLLOW-UP SUPPORT TO CONSTABLES

An over-focus upon the assessment and measurement of past performance is a frequently cited weakness of performance appraisal. It was this retrospective and judgemental focus that prompted Deming's famous attack on performance appraisal (Deming 1982). Therefore, an important issue concerned the extent that sergeants could provide the follow-up training and development anticipated within the espoused model of performance appraisal. Much of this depended upon access to resources for training, but at the same time it also came back to the time available for coaching on the job.

In the first case, there was evidence that the training budget within City Police Service was very constrained, and that even where sergeants had devoted time to identifying development needs for their constables, access to training courses and opportunities for development were not available. With respect to the time constraints upon coaching, the picture was more complex. Partly the increased workloads constrained the time available, and also the performance indicators focused attention on development where performance outputs measured through the computer systems were at stake. At the same time, informal networks proved to be very important sources of development and support.

> ... we don't get much supervision on a daily basis like we used to ...
>
> (Sector Constable 3 – Site 1)

> Sergeants no longer supervise or train PCs. The more senior PCs now do all of this and the sergeants see less of us. We get much less guidance now than in the past.
>
> (Sector Constable 1 – Site 2)

> Of course, if I don't meet their [constables'] needs then we may as well go home. They're more demanding now and question just about everything. They're an intelligent bunch, most have got a degree or some higher education qualification you know. I try and balance what they want with the demands of the PIs [performance indicators] and hope I get it right.
>
> (Relief Sergeant 3 – Site 2)

> The older ones [constables] now give that [support and supervision] to them most of the time because we are stuck inside. Not fair on the PCs and the probationers aren't getting the right level of training any more. My PCs ask me to show them things and I just don't have the time as I'm stuck in Custody all the time.
>
> (Core Sergeant 3 – Site 3)

The sergeants also suffered as development support was not available for them either. In addition, contradictory assumptions governed the internal labour market within the Police Service and recruitment strategies into the service. This was illustrated by a drive in the 1990s to recruit more highly qualified officers. However, they tended to arrive with higher expectations of development opportunities that could not be met within the career structure.

> This is one of my biggest headaches. I cannot get enough courses for them and our local training budget cannot support our own programme for PCs let alone sergeants as well.
>
> (Senior Management Team Member – Site 1)

> I think the idea of continual development is good until you get a few years in, and then you have to ask yourself what value is it to the Police Service? They should be developing themselves for life after [work in City Police Service].
>
> (Senior Management Team Member 1 – Site 1)

PERFORMANCE APPRAISAL AS A LINK BETWEEN ORGANIZATIONAL STRATEGY, SERVICE OBJECTIVES AND INDIVIDUAL BEHAVIOUR

That there should be a seamless link between wider organization objectives and those set in the individual appraisal process is a key assumption that underlies a systems approach to performance management. Yet, this was not upheld by the research findings. During the individual performance appraisal interviews for setting objectives, items were often selected because of their ease of measurement as opposed to their strategic usefulness. It was the divisional indicators based on the performance indicators set centrally by the Audit Commission, Her Majesty's Inspector of Constabulary and the Association of Chief Police Officers that were considered to be the main drivers of performance. Most advocates of a systematic approach to performance management will place equal emphasis upon the line manager role in future work planning and objective setting. However, the evidence indicated that sergeants and their constables perceived the objective setting process as a meaningless ritual that was superseded by a focus upon the performance indicators which had a much greater impact upon the work they did.

> The objectives weren't challenging, and I would have done it anyway. They wouldn't have made a difference to the way I work.
>
> (Relief Constable 1 – Site 1)

> A waste of time as the PIs are the important ones. Why set something that's going to change? It's OK for the theorists in Personnel. They want to get in touch with reality. Things just don't happen like that.
>
> (Sector Sergeant 2 – Site 2)

> The performance indicators have had a great impact on everything I do, and I cannot remember anything else ever having such an impact.
>
> (Sector Sergeant 3 – Site 2)

> We've gone PI barmy and we are concentrating on the minor things rather than the things that matter. I have to do what is measured or I get into trouble. ... It really affects the way we all work. It controls us for most of the time. In some ways it stops us performing because we are chasing the minor things. It needs looking at.
>
> (Relief Sergeant 2 – Site 1)

> The government performance indicators are increasing by the day and most have no relevance to prevention and detection of crime ... In the main they are about providing a façade that gives comfort to the public. A bit like a posh underground station the public can feel safe in while waiting for a train. The problem is the train is running on rickety rails in an unsafe tunnel ... We have a flashy car, pull up at the

scene in minutes, take details and then rush off to the next call. Nothing else happens because we are too busy filling in the forms. Is that really what we are about?

(Sergeant 3 – Stage I Analysis)

Go out and get bodies for whatever we can. Now we just ignore them if they aren't the ones on the objectives. I haven't nicked anyone for possession for ages. We just give a bollocking and destroy the spliff, or whatever. It's crazy!

(Relief Sergeant 3 – Site 1)

Again, senior management were aware of the situation. The impression gained was of a similar ritual going on across sites and functions, which was acknowledged by senior management and constables alike.

Personal ones [objectives] are a pain as most PCs don't see a need for them. I'm not hooked on them, and so I let them pass if the PC says he doesn't want any set. Why bother otherwise?

(Inspector 2 – Site 1)

In many ways it is not of much value because the objectives keep changing and so the relevance a year later is often difficult to measure.

(Inspector 2 – Site 2)

Given the performance indicators, I see less of a need for them [performance objectives]. They no longer have the same objectives over the year because the system changes. No, they need to be thought through again and linked to the PIs.

(Senior Management Team Member 1 – Site 1)

They [sergeants] have less control over their work than anybody. The performance indicators dominate their work.

(Core Constable – Site 1)

Dictates what we do. Measures are used to judge us. If it's not measured, we probably don't do it. The problem is the measures are not necessarily looking at the things which are important to the community.

(Sector Constable 1 – Site 2)

The performance appraisal system was clearly not working in the way it was intended. It was highly bureaucratic, inflexible and time consuming, requiring significant levels of evidence to justify the grading and feedback comments. All energy was focused upon achieving the outcomes set in the divisional performance indicators which relied upon a mixture of computer-generated information and paper processes. What became abundantly clear, was that the performance indicators and not individual performance objectives, were major constraints upon the operational accountability of the sergeants. The impact of the performance indicators was that sergeants undertook those aspects of their work that were measured, relegating other work to secondary importance.

PLAYING THE SYSTEM AND USING INFORMAL PEER GROUP NETWORKS

It is interesting that sergeants found ways of circumventing the system in order to undertake the work that they wanted to do, if it was not part of the approved agenda. The evidence pointed to greater central control over work priorities, but considerable flexibility in how they carried out tasks. It was largely left to the sergeants to decide how to achieve objectives within the constraints of City Police Service policy, relevant legislation and existing resources. However, they drew upon their peer group networks for assistance in this.

> I find that I'm left alone. I think I've got a lot of autonomy – as long as I work within the focused objectives.
>
> (Sector Sergeant 3 – Site 1)

> If I want to do things, I can, provided I justify them under the objectives. It comes back to creative writing. We can do what we like, provided it's within the boundaries they set up. The issue is we have to set it all out within a report. So how we write up the report depends on what we can get away with.
>
> (Relief Sergeant 1 – Site 2)

> The PIs are the way we are measured and they only cover a fraction of what we do on the sector, so we find it frustrating that we are measured on just a small part of our work. ... We have to manipulate the system and find a category that can just about be stretched to meet what we want to do ...
>
> (Sector Constable 3 – Site 1)

> You have a certain amount of peer pressure and learn from others who perform well in a particular field. Once I reach that level I try to develop it further. We are an organization that reacts to peer pressure. We work together to resolve issues and support one another – create bureaucratic systems to stop doing the things we don't want to do ... that's from peer pressure.
>
> (Sector Sergeant 1 – Site 1)

> The older sergeants don't like it because I won't bow to them and do things their way ... We younger ones stick together as we are the future and will have to work together longer ...
>
> (Sector Sergeant 3 – Site 1)

In particular, this 'network effect' and influence of the peer group of sergeants provided a means of getting round the constraints of performance management. While the greatest influence (especially in a pseudo-military bureaucracy like the Police Service) might be expected to come from the immediate manager – the inspector –

surprisingly this was not the case. Peer group sergeants, and to a lesser extent, the constables reporting into the sergeants determined what got done. This was particularly the case with the younger generation of sergeants. The inspectors influenced the prioritization of tasks, but not how they were actually carried out. Even more interesting was the perception that these developments had increased since the introduction of the NPM. The 'canteen culture' had clearly survived.

In principle, the performance management system should have enabled sergeants to exercise greater operational autonomy. In reality this was constrained by the volume of work and the combination of the performance indicators and the new computer systems. However, for the sector sergeants at both sites, and the relief sergeants at Site 1, there was more flexibility about *how* they undertook their work, even though the CAD and CRIS systems and the performance indicators reduced their autonomy over *what* had to be done.

DISCUSSION AND CONCLUSION

The overall impression gained from this study was that the introduction of new methods of individual performance appraisal was placing police sergeants under considerable pressure, yet, paradoxically this may not have resulted in improved performance. There are a number of reasons for this. Most importantly, the new performance appraisal system was being introduced alongside major changes in the sergeants' role – changes that were giving rise to role conflict because of the competing demands of their jobs. They were still expected to take a key role in operational policing, but at the same time were increasingly expected to distance themselves from operations and their team in order to supervise, manage and lead. They also faced role strain because of the discrepancy between the information and resources available to them, and those required for effective performance. It was clear that this placed constraints upon the effective operation of the performance appraisal system. This reinforces the argument made earlier by Holloway *et al.* (1999) that complex approaches to performance management are only as good as the people who apply them and the context in which they are applied. Similarly, it supports the earlier work of Stiles *et al.* (1997) and Harris (2001) emphasizing the negative effect of the lack of incentives and training opportunities, and the short-term focus and lack of time, on achieving effective performance management

Second, the pressures for increased accountability by means of performance appraisal linked to the performance indicators set in the strategic plan may well have backfired. Not only did this encourage a focus upon *output* rather than *outcome*, but it also encouraged manipulating the system, and evasion. The strong internal labour market within City Police Service, and the attendant 'canteen culture' created a strong informal network of peers and constables that determined what got done. Sergeants and their constables identified strongly with their 'sector' or 'relief'. Paradoxically, their immediate line manager, the inspector, appeared to have little influence over what got done, reinforcing the traditional 'us-and-them' mentality.

Third, these findings on individual performance appraisals have implications for wider performance management systems. One of the major precepts of performance management, namely accountability, could not be enhanced, lending support to Power's argument (1997) that formalized control systems have more to do with sustaining a myth of control and external legitimization, than with any real improvements in operational performance. Other research (Strebler *et al.* 2001) has shown that too close an alignment between individual performance appraisal and organizational strategy might provide a clear 'line of sight', but the apparent rational and linear logic that individual and organizational goals can be aligned, is flawed. Frequent changes of department, and individual objectives, and organizational politics are a more likely outcome. This research has also shown how important the environmental context is within which performance management is implemented. The demands and expectations of other stakeholders and members of role sets, and resource constraints appear to be key factors influencing the implementation of systematic performance management.

Finally, the stereotypical polarization between 'bureaucracy' and 'management', which is implicitly at the heart of the New Public Management, is undermined when subject to closer examination. The introduction of the NPM within City Police Service, and its attendant performance management system had clearly led to more detailed scrutiny and paperwork, formal recentralization of control and attempts to constrain operational autonomy. Yet this study has shown that many aspects of the NPM were not working as intended. For example, the political control of resources meant that centralist performance indicators were used to control the activities of sergeants. The consequence of this was that sergeants and their constables were unable to display the flexibility, customer focus and leadership and entrepreneurial behaviours extolled by the advocates of the NPM. At the same time, this research has shown that the implications of centralist control also generate an environment ripe for dysfunctional behaviour. Informal networks became the primary means of getting things done. Finally, the application of generic standardized performance indicators adversely affected the ability of sergeants to react to local issues and demands effectively. The inference is that due to the differences in organizational goals, environments, structures and managerial values, it may well be impossible to implement NPM techniques successfully in a public sector 'essential' service such as the Police Service. Research elsewhere in Australia (Vickers and Kouzmin 2001: 20) reinforces the conclusion of this article that 'police organisations . . . do not lend themselves comfortably to economic ideals, scientific emphases and efficiency "panaceas" offered by managerialist theory and consultancy firms'. There is much scope for further research within the police and other 'essential' services, to determine whether this is a general finding.

REFERENCES

Ackroyd, S., Hughes, J. A. and Soothill, K. (1989) 'Public Sector Services and Their Management'. *Journal of Management Studies*, 26:6 pp603 – 19.

Armstrong, M. and Barron, A. (1998) *Performance Management: The New Realities*, London: Institute of Personnel and Development.

Audit Commission (1995) *Management Handbook: Paying the Piper. . . . Calling the Tune*, London: HMSO, cited in Mwita, J. 'Performance Management Model: A Systems-Based Approach to Public Service Quality'. *International Journal of Public Sector Management*, 13:1 pp19 – 37.

Boland, T. and Fowler, A. (2000) 'A Systems Perspective of Performance Management in Public Sector Organisations'. *International Journal of Public Sector Management*, 13:5 pp417 – 46.

Boxall, P. and Purcell, J. (2003) *Strategy and Human Resource Management*, Basingstoke: Palgrave.

Boyne, G. A. (2002) 'Public and Private Management: What's the Difference?'. *Journal of Management Studies*, 39:1 pp97 – 122.

Butterfield, R. (2001) 'The Introduction of New Public Management in the Police Service: Its Impact on the Role of the Police Sergeant Supervisor'. Unpublished PhD Thesis, Kingston University.

Carter, N., Klein, R. and Day, P. (1995) *How Organisations Measure Success: The Use of Performance Indicators in* 'The Role of Expectations in the Perception of Health Care Quality: Developing a Conceptual Model'. *International Journal of Health Care Quality Assurance*, 10:3 pp131 – 40.

Conway, T. and Wilcocks, S. (1997) 'The Role of Expectations in the Perception of Health Care Quality: Developing a Conceptual Model'. *International Journal of Health Care Quality Assurance*, 10:3 pp 131 – 40.

Cope, S., Leishman, F. and Starie, P. (1997) 'Globalisation, New Public Management and the Enabling State'. *International Journal of Public Sector Management*, 10:6 pp444 – 60.

Deming, W. E. (1982) *Out of the Crisis*, Boston, MA: MIT Press.

Ferlie, E. (1992) 'The Creation and Evolution of Quasi-Markets in the Public Sector: A Problem for Strategic Management'. *Strategic Management Journal*, 13 pp79 – 97.

Ferlie, E. and Pettigrew, A. (1996) 'Managing through Networks: Some Issues and Implications for the NHS'. Special Issue of *British Journal of Management*, 7 ppS81 – S99.

Flynn, N. (1997) *Public Sector Management* (3rd edn), London: Prentice Hall.

Fondas, N. and Stewart, R. (1994) 'Enactment in Managerial Jobs: A Role Analysis'. *Journal of Management Studies*, 31:1 pp83 – 103.

Graef, R. (1989) *Talking Blues: The Police in Their Own Words*, London: Collins Harvill.

Harris, L. (2001) 'Rewarding Employee Performance: Line Managers' Values, Beliefs and Perspectives'. *International Journal of Human Resource Management*, 12:2 pp1182 – 92.

Harrow, J. and Shaw, M. (1992) 'The Manager Faces the Customer' in L. Wilcocks and J. Harrow (eds) *Rediscovering Public Services Management*. Maidenhead: McGraw-Hill.

HMSO (1993a) *Inquiry into Police Responsibilities and Rewards*, Home Office, Northern Ireland Office & Scottish Office, London: HMSO.

————— (1993b) *Police Reform*, Home Office White Paper, London: HMSO.

Hoggett, P. (1996) 'New Modes of Control in the Public Service'. *Public Administration*, 74:1 pp9 – 32.

Holloway, J., Francis, G. and Hinton, M. (1999) 'A Vehicle for Change? A Case Study of Performance Improvement in the "New" Public Sector'. *International Journal of Public Sector Management*, 12:4 pp351 – 65.

Hood, C. (1991) 'A Public Management for All Seasons?'. *Public Administration*, 69:1 p 3 – 19.

Horton, S. and Farnham, D. (eds) (1999) *Public Management in Britain*, Basingstoke: Macmillan.

Katz, D. and Kahn, R. L. (1978) *The Social Psychology of Organisations* (2nd edn), New York: Wiley.

Machin, J. L. J. (1981) 'The Expectation Approach' in J. L. J. Machin, R. Stewart and C. Hales (eds) *Towards Managerial Effectiveness: Applied Research Perspectives on the Managerial Task*. Farnborough: Gower.

Mark, A. and Scott, H. (1992) 'Management of the National Health Service' in L. Willcocks and J. Harrow (eds) *Rediscovering Public Services Management*. Maidenhead: MacGraw-Hill.

Merton, R. K. (1957) *Social Theory and Social Structure* (revised edn). Glencoe, IL: Free Press.

Mohrman, A. M. and Mohrman, S. A. (1995) 'Performance Management Is Running the Business'. *Compensation and Benefits Review*, July – August pp 69 – 75.

Nutley, S. (2000) 'Beyond Systems: HRM Audits in the Public Sector'. *Human Resource Management Journal*, 10:2 21 – 38.

Peck, J (1994) 'Organisational Behaviour in the MPS'. Unpublished MPhil Thesis, Exeter University.

Pollitt, C. (1993) *Managerialism and the Public Services: The Anglo-American Experience*, London: Macmillan.

Poole, M. R, Boyne, G. and Mendes, P. (2002) 'Public and Private Sector Managers: A Test of the "Convergence Thesis" Based on Cross Sectoral and Longitudinal Data'. *British Academy of Management Annual Conference Proceedings*, University of Middlesex, September.

Power, M. (1997) *The Audit Society: Rituals of Verification*, Oxford: Oxford University Press.

Purcell, J., Kinnie, N., Hutchinson, S., Rayton, B. and Swart, J. (2003) *Understanding the People and Performance Link: Unlocking the Black Box*, London: Chartered Institute of Personnel and Development.

Reiner, R. (1985) *The Politics of the Police*, Brighton: Harvester Press.

Rhodes, R. A. W. (1994) 'The Hollowing Out of the State: The Changing Nature of the Public Service in Britain'. *Political Quarterly*, 65:2 pp138 – 51.

Rouse, J. (1999) 'Performance Management, Quality Management and Contracts' in S. Horton and D. Farnham (eds) *Public Management in Britain*. Basingstoke: Macmillan.

Savage, S. P. and Leishman, F. (1996) 'Managing the Police: A Force for Change' in D. Farnham and S. Horton (eds) *Managing the New Public Services*. Basingstoke: Macmillan.

Smith, P. (1995) 'Performance Indicators and Outcomes in the Public Sector'. *Public Money and Management*, 15:4 pp13 – 16.

Stiles, P., Gratton, L., Truss, C., Hope-Hailey, V. and McGovern, P. (1997) 'Performance Management and the Psychological Contract'. *Human Resource Management Journal*, 7:1 pp57 – 66.

Strauss, A. and Corbin, J. (1998) *Basics of Qualitative Research*, London: Sage Publications.

Strebler, M., Robinson, D. and Bevan, S. (2001) 'Performance Review: Balancing Objectives and Content'. *IES Report* no. 370. Brighton: Institute of Employment Studies.

Tonge, R. and Horton, S. (1996) 'Financial Management' in D. Farnham and S. Horton (eds) *Managing the New Public Services*. Basingstoke: Macmillan.

Truss, C. (2001) 'Complexities and Controversies in Linking HRM with Organizational Outcomes.' *Journal of Management Studies*, 38:8 pp1121 – 49.

Tsui, A. S. (1984a) 'A Multiple-Constituency Framework of Managerial Reputational Effectiveness' in J. G. Hunt, C. A. Hoskin, C. Schriesheim and R. Stewart (eds) *Leadership*. New York: Pergamon.

——— (1984b) 'A Role Set Analysis of Managerial Reputation' in *Organizational Behaviour and Human Performance*. New York: Academic Press.

Vickers, M. H. and Kouzmin, A. (2001) 'New Managerialism and Australian Police Organisations: A Cautionary Research Note'. *International Journal of Public Sector Management*, 14:1 pp7 – 26.

SUPPORTING INTER-ORGANIZATIONAL PARTNERSHIPS IN THE PUBLIC SECTOR

The role of joined up action learning and research

Pete Mann, Sue Pritchard and Kirstein Rummery

PARTNERSHIP WORKING AND THE WELFARE STATE

As part of its review of the public sector (Powell 1999), New Labour has attempted to find a 'Third Way' (Giddens 1998) to deliver health and social care services in the UK (Jessop 2000), characterized as 'governance' (Rhodes 1997; Stoker 2000): 'self-organising, inter-organisational networks' (Rhodes 1997: 53) which promise locally responsive services with the state acting as an 'enabler' rather than a direct provider of services (Newman 2001). Part of the rhetoric of this approach is epitomized by the emphasis New Labour places on 'partnership' working – Jupp found the term 'partnership' used over 6,000 times in Parliament during 1999 as compared to 38 times in 1989 (Jupp 2000). But this situation is not unique to the UK context: partnership working, particularly between health and social care and area-based initiatives focusing on tackling social exclusion, are proliferating within the European Union (Geddes and Benington 2001), as well as within Nordic, Commonwealth and North American welfare regimes (Bradford 2003; Considine and Lewis 2003; Ovretveit 2003).

Within the current policy context, partnership working is encouraged between the public and private sector, the public and voluntary sector, the state and the individual and between statutory sectors (Balloch and Taylor 2001; Glendinning *et al.* 2002; Ling 2002), where there is commonality of interest and a history of failure to co-ordinate services effectively (Audit Commission 1998) – again not just in the UK. Various welfare regimes on the Continent, across the Atlantic and in the Antipodes have adopted 'Third Way' type approaches to the governance of welfare delivery (Considine and Lewis 2003; Papadopoulos 2003). Within the sphere of health and social care in the UK, it has moved from being a marginal activity to being a mainstream effort upon which the relevant agencies are now regularly scrutinized and audited (Boyne *et al.* 2003; Cameron and Lart 2003) – a form of 'statutory voluntarism' (Paton 1999).

The discourse of partnership appears to be becoming a ubiquitous feature of the welfare landscape (who could object to the principle of partnership? – Clarke and Glendinning 2002) such that it has become a hegemonic term. However, a stress on partnerships can be a neat way of deflecting attention away from the failure of welfare agencies to attain core objectives of meeting users' needs (Rummery 2002), and there is scant evidence that efforts to improve partnership working in the public sector result in improved outcomes for service users (Ling 2002; Cameron and Lart 2003). In some sectors, partnership working can in fact lead to net losses for less powerful partners, particularly for the voluntary sector (Craig *et al.* 2002), raising the concern that partnerships may at best result in neutral outcomes for users and at worst in poorer outcomes than other ways of delivering welfare (Rummery 2002). There are also concerns about partnership working within the context of welfare governance that call into question their democratic legitimacy and their accountability to users in the face of powerful vested interests (Craig *et al.* 2002; Papadopoulos 2003; Pettigrew 2003).

Nevertheless, the demand for partnership working in the public sector means there is no shortage of ways to conceptualize and measure it (Asthana *et al.* 2002; Powell and Exworthy 2002; Sullivan and Skelcher 2002). One analysis of welfare partnerships across a range of settings, including education, health, social care, urban regeneration and criminal justice policy in the UK has found that what distinguishes it from other ways of joint working is two things (Rummery 2002). First, the partners involved had to have a significant degree of *interdependence* – they had to rely on each other in order to achieve their own core objectives, and all partners involved had to recognize this interdependence (Audit Commission 1998). Second, what makes a relationship a partnership, as opposed to a contractual or other type of joint working arrangement, is that the agencies or individuals involved are engaged in a relationship based on *trust* (Huxham 2000). When these two elements are in place, the evidence suggests that interorganizational partnerships can evolve and develop to meet the challenge of delivering health and social care services in a constantly shifting welfare environment (Hudson 2000; Balloch and Taylor 2001; Rummery and Coleman 2003).

NEW POLICIES, NEW CHALLENGES, NEW PARTNERSHIPS

Within the UK, New Labour has focused on reviewing the way in which the National Health Service is structured and managed. One of the earliest shifts in policy announced after it first came to power in 1997 was the publication of *The New NHS: Modern, Dependable* (Secretary of State for Health 1997), which announced the formation of Primary Care Trusts (PCTs) in which general practitioners and community nurses work alongside managers and representatives from local social services department to influence the commissioning of healthcare services for their area.

The formation of these new Primary Care Trusts means that new kinds of health and social care partnerships are developing that involve new actors requiring new skills and knowledge. General practitioners are having to learn how to (a) commission services for their local population rather than for their individual patients, (b) undertake this process collaboratively with other health colleagues; and (c) work with outside agencies such as social services departments. Historically, general practitioners, fundamentally important to the National Health Service, have occupied a strange position in the UK public sector: largely independent contractors, they are encouraged to act as competitive small businesses rather than as public sector employees. The challenge of commissioning services collaboratively within a localized health economy is therefore a difficult one for groups of professionals with no supported history of partnership working (Calnan and Gabe 2001; Harrison and Dowswell 2002). Social services workers, also at the frontline, are similarly on a steep learning curve with regards to partnerships within the new Primary Care Trusts. They have had to learn quickly how primary care works and the pattern of services available within their local healthcare economy (Coleman and Rummery 2003). Community nurses have had to adapt to their new status as 'purchasers', contrasted with their earlier status as 'providers' under the previous administration's marketized community-care system where they were usually excluded from decisions about commissioning services. The same has been true for managers and administrators of frontline services and for practitioners and leaders of voluntary bodies contributing to welfare provision. For all these professionals, the new ways of integrated working have called for accelerated ways of relevant learning.

Frontline practitioners in health and social care have therefore had to cope with two fundamentally new and difficult challenges. First, they have had to adapt to changes within their own organization, its aims, values, structures and governance. Often these have threatened their own professional status, job security and service provision. Second, they have found that the political commitment to partnership working has meant that the onus of delivering it has fallen directly on them. Partnership working is no longer an optional add-on, confined to special projects or limited areas. It has become a fundamental part of the mainstream daily work for many frontline health and social care professionals and managers (Coppel and Dyas 2003).

SUPPORTING NEW JOINT WORKING IN ORGANIZATIONAL UPHEAVAL

There is always a danger that structural turbulence will result in organizations becoming inward-focused, coping with their new obligations alongside unfamiliar managerial structures, and that the professionals working within those new structures will concentrate inwardly on their practice, protecting themselves from job insecurity and new stresses and strains from upheavals (Miller and Ahmad 2000). The evidence from studies of the implementation of *The New NHS* and the NHS Plan suggests that partnership working between health and social care did suffer in the first few years: organization turbulence and the need to create new managerial structures deflected managers' delivering on their new obligations (Glendinning *et al.* 2001; Rummery 2004). A key question is therefore how to support managers and frontline workers in gaining the necessary knowledge and new skills to develop and sustain interorganiza-tional and interprofessional partnerships in this climate of change (Hudson *et al.* 1997; Sullivan and Skelcher 2002).

The need for joint working is clear. In the face of ample evidence for the *interdependence* of health and social care, both sides have been accused in the UK of failing to co-ordinate services, wasting resources by duplicating assessments and overusing acute and residential care owing to not investing in low-level, preventive services (Secretary of State for Health 2000). And this despite interdependency being enshrined in statute (Paton 1999). Nevertheless, while interdependency may be an espoused 'given' between health and social care, *trust* is not. The organizational barriers to joint working, which include differing aims, priorities, funding cycles and accountability arrangements, have been made worse by a history of cost-shunting and blame-shifting between the two sectors. In addition, health and social care frontline workers have interprofessional barriers to contend with when trying to work in partnership: managers, doctors, general practitioners, nurses and social workers all have very different professional values, models and jargon which can be difficult to overcome without extraordinary patience and a true sense of shared goals. Both of these qualities are exacerbated when under pressure, which for frontline practitioners is most working days.

The evidence from the early years of joint working under New Labour indicates that interprofessional and interorganizational trust is possible (Balloch and Taylor 2001). Trust develops from the experience of working together successfully and from overcoming interprofessional mistrust that is usually based on a lack of knowledge about each other's value assumptions, priorities and ways of working. It is supported by shared goals, commitment, honesty and the ability of individuals and organizations to learn constructively from mistakes and failures. It relies on key individuals being willing to take risks and 'think outside the box' – moving away from accepted ways of working in organizational silos.

Given the continuing pressure on frontline health and social care staff to deliver on the partnership agenda, how can they be helped to develop the capacities needed to engage with their partners interdependently and trustingly? The remainder of this article will examine evidence from an action learning and research programme to see whether this work-led emphasis in continuing professional development can support partnership working in the public sector.

NEW MANAGEMENT DEVELOPMENT?

As the landscape of health and social care was changing, so was the map of the territory of management learning (Senge 1990; Pedler *et al.* 1991; Burgoyne and Reynolds 1997). A whole-systems approach to conceptualizing organization, manifested in the move towards partnerships in the public sector (Attwood *et al.* 2003) and towards networks and alliances in the private (Dixon 2000), saw new forms of individual and institutional learning emerge to mirror the New Public Management. Management education in the 1980s and 1990s became characterized, *inter alia*, by a polarization between competency frameworks – tightly structured approaches to prescriptive skills progression irrespective of context – and more process-orientated, situated enquiry emphasizing expanded knowledge within the organization. The latter typically hinged on less tangible, more tacit approaches to enhancing professional consciousness and corporate capacity. Of particular interest within the workplace were creating conversions in organizational knowledge (Nonaka and Takeuchi 1995), embracing complexity and uncertainty in systems (Morgan 1986; Zimmerman *et al.* 1998), and transcending reductionist rationality with multiple streams of intelligence (Goleman

1996; Cooper and Sawaf 1998; Lewin and Regine 1999; Zohar and Marshall 2000). Both prescriptive and emergent ends of a continuum pressed upon human resource development (HRD) practices in health and social care. This left professionals on the ground confronted with choice, contradiction – and confusion.

An example would be a 1994 action learning programme for NHS human resources (HR) personnel in London (much smaller and less ambitious than the first action learning initiative in the capital's health system three decades earlier – see Wieland and Bradford 1981). It was intended to support HR professionals in rising to the challenge of the radical changes anticipated in the health sector. That it was commissioned by the then NHS Management Executive confirmed the historical frustration within the service of too much management training – too often uni-disciplinary, uni-agency and uni-focused – doing too little to prepare practitioners and managers for the enormous gestalt of changes in organizational performance demanded of them (NHSME 1991; Attwood 1994). One outcome of the programme for an HR director on it was contracting a local university to offer a taught Masters' programme with action learning in it for frontline staff in his own, rapidly changing organization. Two years on, two evaluations – one internal, the other by the NHS Training Directorate – raised concerns, the chief of which was confusion in learning agendas. The local Trust and its employees had assumed they were signing up to a developmental approach (emphasis on process), but had found the university delivering subject matter (emphasis on content). Underpinning values of each stakeholder were conflicting: participants wanting *support* to experience, test out and practise partnership, the institution aiming to *teach* its abstracted meaning. The lack of congruence between client needs and provider methods diminished the value for participants and reduced the gains for the organization.

So just what is action learning? How does it address intractable challenges by empowering resourcefulness in those who know, who care and who can (Revans 1982)? How does it help managers and practitioners learn deliberately 'with and from each other' through a process of actually doing something to make a difference? Action learning in HRD terms is work- and experience-led, as contrasted with 'instruction-led' learning (Drake 1995). Learning begins with inquiry into real problems for which there are no known solutions, involves others in rigorous review of progress and demands accountable action. 'Learning is cradled in the task', was how its founder put it (Revans 1983), always distinguishing 'between getting something done and talking about getting it done'. Revans was an Olympic athlete (as well as astrophysicist and first professor of industrial administration in Britain) and was fond of pointing out the difference 'between consulting past reports on the Olympic Games to decide that one may need to clear 2m 40 to win the next high jump . . . and . . . actually sailing over that height in the crowded stadium' (Revans 1983: 7).

Critics of the action learning method to develop managers assert that 'the rationally based action learning cycle encourages a self-limiting perspective on learning and change for individuals and organizations' (Vince and Martin 1993: 214). They suggest this deficiency can be overcome through introducing models of emotional and political dimensions of organizational life. A summary (Pedler 1997) of frequently heard criticisms of action learning include that it:

- increasingly is incorporated unthinkingly within management agendas;
- is atheoretical;
- is too centred on the individual as agent; and
- can degenerate, through its core mechanism of action learning sets (peer groups for scrutinizing each other's work), into support groups for individuals.

Recent growth in the action learning approach has also led to a proliferation of any small group activity coming to bear its name. The design of management learning called action learning has not been precise, as when educational institutions 'provide' it to client systems. As a result, a dilution of rigour in practice has been observed (Boot and Reynolds 1997) – a criticism attributed to the small action learning programme referred to earlier and to others (Pritchard 2003). Perhaps action learning is one of those things in HRD that is simple but not easy?

The review of the north-west London action learning initiative in the mid-1990s made one thing obvious: all the earlier needs and challenges of system upheaval in the health and social care sector were still around and growing:

- rapid integration of community trusts: some were already merging and changing their patterns of service on the ground;
- forced shifts into Primary Care Trusts: the slower pace of change had been removed centrally;
- localization of professional working: primary-care led and patient-focused service meant smaller, local multi-disciplinary teams – contrasted with the previous recent growth of vertical professional hierarchies;
- new partnerships with social services: the joined up/seamless-service mantra now required strategic and functional relationships with social care;
- formal qualifications driving HR: recognized, post-registration training was increasingly linked to key staff shortages, to attainment of government targets and to service debates on job design – all of which risked neglect of harder-to-measure, continuous, less formal learning on the job.

The complex and fast-changing territory of joint working urgently required greater flexibility on the ground; so did the training of its change leaders for their learning to be relevant and any academic recognition of it robust. Traditionally taught coursework, even when part-time, was not meeting the multi-disciplinary requirements of health and social care professionals who were now working across customary endpoints enshrined as 'boundary spanning'. They criticized their postgraduate programmes for instructing them in classrooms away from work, for 'pushing content information as sufficient to act on', for 'focusing on what I *had done* versus . . . what I am going to do'. Their MBA provision fared no better: 'global . . . but not relevant', with 'very little impact on my role as a manager', were ways these boundary-spanning professionals and managers criticized academia's relentless provision of information 'in silos' (Mann 2003b).

JOINED UP LEARNING IN PARTNERSHIP

What was called for to improve joined up working, it was now clearer than ever, was joined up learning. This 'new' kind of management development would need to respect an old principle of human progress: real challenges of working in new ways drive relevant learning in behaving differently. And if this management development were to be accredited, assessment requirement would need to be based wholly in the practitioners' efforts to join up their real work. If there were to be academic input, it would need to derive entirely from requirements arising out of the challenge of that work. And if this real work were to be so demanding, something more than abstract understanding of its nature would have to be supported. How could joined up learning and enquiry enable practitioners from different backgrounds systematically to link day-to-day real experience with their personal growth and continued professional development in ways which both mirrored their working reality yet released them temporarily from its disabling grip?

To learn in ways leading to formal qualifications which integrated academic assessment within real work and blended personal insight with organizational knowledge would require two complementary yet distinct kinds of learning skills. One would be skill in learning *about* professional and administrative matters in changing systems, things already largely known for solving real problems 'out there'. This skill would help practitioners update and understand the meaning of changes in legislation, in organizational blueprints, in modes of professional practice. However, this skill would have to be joined up with another for learning personal, harder-to-recognize-and-own things 'in here' about oneself as a practising change agent working with others from different professions. This skill would take one determined to influence others into discovering significant unknowns, like that they might be a part of the problem in the first place or that they do not even know in the first place they ought to be discovering this. Action learning, not a 'new' form of management development, acknowledged both these interlinked learning skills.

Action learning requires 'programmed knowledge' (P) as well as 'questioning insight' (Q) (Revans 1983). The former kind of learning (P) recognizes the importance of that which is known and is wise to learn: relevant retrievable information, evidence from research, content from a syllabus, an idea in a text – things established as good practice or good sense. For a practitioner to inform their thinking and gain from P, skill is required to discern, articulate and make sense of previously existing information. This is the learning skill emphasized in academia. But the other kind of learning (Q) demands a different kind of skill. The ability to pose fresh questions out of hunches or ignorance requires affective and social competence in broaching and engaging that which is unknown or less certain. Q is more associated with serendipitous exploration ('Ready. Fire. Aim') than with orthodox prescription ('Ready. Aim. Fire' – the logic of P). Q is the off-road meandering of stochastic query ('What would happen if . . .?'), not the main thoroughfare of studious analysis (If x equals income and y equals . . .' – again the drill of P). Hence in action learning, the well-known learning equation: L (learning) = P + Q.

In the current changing landscape of health and social care provision, there was much P in interorganizational partnership waiting for skilful learning: new policy documents, fresh legal obligations, changing organizational arrangements, re-cast professional values, priorities and procedures. There was also an abundance of Q that demanded skill in learning the less 'knowable' and the more implicit dimensions behind actual practice in joint working. These included historically challenging 'people management' areas of interpersonal and political competence needed for collaborating (with parties who might have let you down in the past) and for establishing a relationship (with a person whom you may see as exploiting change for personal gain). These are the skills for taking calculated risks (to put your idea – or yourself – forward when unsure) and for persisting when others don't want to know (relentlessly asking, 'What about the patient?').

It was concerns over these on a practical level in Spring 1999 that found a meeting of HR personnel in health and social care in north-west London trying to secure commitment to return to the essence of action learning to improve partnership practice. A commissioning consortium of health authority and trust HR directors and social services training managers began seeking funding from the NHS Executive and the Education Consortium. This process of jointly commissioning what was to be called JULIP – joined up learning in partnership – quickly illustrated core challenges in practising partnership. The health side, for example, was experiencing fairly commonly understood structural change in which social care partners were slow to engage. Social services members on the new Project Team, from the standpoint of health representatives, would be signalling participation in principle yet take too much time to produce participants on the programme. JULIP quickly shaped into a multi-agency, multi-professional action learning and research programme open to those who could benefit from it and make a contribution to systemic learning (including non-degree holders, unusual in the research world). Regular meetings of action learning sets, comprising micro-interprofessional partnerships of three to seven members, would be a key structure: each small group would meet once a month as accountable 'good company' (Morris 1987) to review and plan how each member was getting on in between meetings to make a difference on real problems in real time with real people (Revans 1983).

In April 2000 the first cohort of eighteen participants from diverse backgrounds began, followed in the Spring of 2001 by fourteen more and then six in that September. With attrition and a fourth cohort of thirteen in September 2002, programme numbers soon stood at thirty-eight – five of these in and out of NGOs during the time. Attrition was never straightforward (leaving public service altogether/ changing an entire way of life) and reduced the original eighteen to twelve for redistribution into two sets – with three participants later returning to form their own set. Each participant registered for three years at the Revans Institute for Action Learning and Research at the University of Salford, part-time for an MSc by research. A 50,000-word dissertation would account for the improvement at work and the learning behind that. Action-based studies soon ran the gamut of partnership practice – below a sample of research topics:

- Managing change, collaboration and integration in a PCT.
- Coping with the nebulous, bringing organizations together to provide zero-tolerance service.
- Working across organizational boundaries to improve health outcomes for people with learning disabilities.
- Welfare advocacy in local government partnership.
- Development of interdisciplinary service within a child development centre.
- Partnership working and empowering older people to influence decision making and service delivery.

While attracting top-level support, JULIP still got funds 'on a wing and a prayer': some senior health service managers boldly used NHS funds to support people employed by social service departments; others paid fees three years up front to circumvent later policy changes. JULIP's funding remained constrained as more decisions taken centrally on training strategies and budgets furthered eroded HRD autonomy at local level. By the end of 2002, JULIP's Project Team needed evidence – however limited – to justify whether this different approach to supporting joint working was making a difference to interorganizational professionals and their employers. A small evaluation was commissioned. Between late June and mid-July 2003, seven JULIP sets comprising twenty-eight of the scheme's thirty-eight participants were visited to find out what 'individuals do differently . . . where new knowledge has been created . . . [and] the demonstration of new thinking' (Evaluation Buzz Group Report to Project Team 2003). In five of the seven research visits, the evaluation was the only item on the day's agenda: informants took it in turns to talk about JULIP as the evaluator took notes. At the two other meetings, each set proceeded with its own agenda with the evaluator asking questions at the end.

The field study was seeking self-reported evidence of whether action learning enabled busy career professionals under pressure to change their interorganizational practice, but could not include views of the many people they worked with outside of the learning sets. During the seven visits, few specific questions were asked by the evaluator after the initial one of, 'What and who are joined up in JULIP?' Data gathering in the main proceeded by pursuing things previously referred to by informants: 'Can you relate that to JULIP?', 'So are you saying the set helps you to learn?', 'It sounds like the experience in JULIP has affected your performance on a number of levels ...?' Examples were continuously sought about the professional's unique experience. When not forthcoming it was often provided by someone else – an indicator of high interprofessional knowledge among set members? Sampling in the field was to find out if JULIP had 'distinctive characteristics' (Mann 2003a): no leading questions were ever asked about confidence, openness, trust, etc.

In October 2003, a 42-page report to the Project Team (Mann 2003b) concluded there were distinctions. (Below, Roman numerals after a quotation refer to which fieldvisit [I – VII] and Arabic numbers to which set member was offered a view [1 – 6] at the meeting.):

•   JULIP strengthened diverse outcomes, from emotional to behavioural, in continuing personal and professional growth to drive institutional change:

We are developing ourselves and not just skills: developing the person to go along with the skill.

(IV, 3)

•   JULIP's work-led action research emphasis structured essential interplay in experience-based leadership training between 'engaging task' and 'thinking strategically about task':

we sat within our own work [the set] exploring what partnerships meant to us and raising lots and lots of questions that I would have never thought of.

(VII, 5)

•   JULIP's developmental mode of regular action learning set meetings helped convert specialist expertise and day-to-day goodwill into longer-term career and cross-sector contributions:

JULIP has stopped us from working on an island.

(III, 3)

•   JULIP made central campaigns like Improving Working Lives a reality by bolstering collegial respect through the constructive exchange of its small, dutiful, mixed-sector action learning sets:

> The set is incredibly positive for my own self-esteem ... The fact that people I respect [set colleagues] say, 'You are better than that', means a *great* deal more than from a line manager.
>
> (VI, 2)

From these summary findings, though, key questions remained: does joined up action learning and research specifically contribute to the two distinctive characteristics of joint working identified earlier: interdependence and trust? Are action learning sets a particularly suitable crucible for strengthening these twin benchmarks of inter-organizational partnerships? The learning equation previewed above provided a useful frame for pursuing these questions in the current study:

Learning = P (programmed knowledge)

+

Q (questioning insight).

Our working hypothesis became:

Effective joint working in JULIP = skill to strengthen *interdependence (P)*: recognizing inter-reliance in practice by learning things largely already known

+

skill to renew *trust (Q)*: learning things more subtle and elusive for engaging the unknown (behaving openly, 'thinking outside the box', etc.).

The analysis presented below under the two elements of the learning equation remains grounded in data from the seven field visits: over 10,000 words of hand-taken notes from nineteen hours of talking among twenty-one women and seven men in JULIP in mid-2003. The previous interaction of these professionals over the months in dozens of their small set meetings was providing them, in methodological terms, with a 'certain *type* of data': 'relatively short-term' sequences of 'repetitive' behaviour 'easily reported upon' (Brown 1973). These data would be selected into the present study for constant analytic comparison (Glaser 1978) based on how problematic (Spencer and Dale 1979), how recurrent and how energetic their manifestations appeared during the visit to the evaluator as the informant made reference to them. If there was energy behind their self-report, or other sets had referred to similar contentious issues, the data would earn their way into the analysis.

The original analysis in the report to the Project Team (Mann 2003b) had proceeded inductively to illuminative distinctive characteristics of the action scene (Partlett and Hamilton 1972; Locke 2001). No attention had been given then to the theoretical debate around interorganizational partnerships (because the Project Team didn't want a discourse they were familiar with). The current co-authored academic article previews key conceptual variables (interdependence and trust) which *ex post facto* are now taken account of within the original analysis. These two factors in turn have been theoretically elaborated with action learning's twin elements of P and Q. In progressing from open immersion into data (fieldstudy) to a later hypothesis of an interrelationship (this article), the research approach has paralleled the way practice generally develops: from experience to understanding (Mann 1999). It has also had the methodological effect of elevating the research approach in the present study to the status of a 'chronological lie' (Collins 1979): plausibly suggesting now a possible 'solution' to a problem whose complexity was not fully appreciated by the field evaluator at the time. What follows, therefore, is based in what individuals presented at ground-level, not on the Project Team's comprehensive appreciation of the wider issues they grappled with throughout the life of the project.

DIFFERENTIATING INTERDEPENDENCE: THE SKILL OF P IN JOINED UP ACTION LEARNING

P as a skill in action learning for strengthening interdependence can be seen when practitioners refer to occupational sectors they previously were out of date with or biased against. JULIP releases a positive disposition to differentiate 'where people are coming from, what language they're using' (VII, 2):

> You can recognize a social services or health sector practitioner from the moment they open their mouth. Health service personnel come to the point ... [whereas social care practitioners] are inhibited from saying what they think. If the person starts with a pre-amble, they're from social services. They're so used to build-ups ... because they work to different standards, regulations, statutory control, ... [In health] We feel a greater freedom of thought ... [But] They can't be that free thinking.
>
> (I, 1)

This helps one appreciate interdependence: 'The speed within local authority and within health is very different: a local authority takes a longer view, seeks more information, does not rush in. It needs time to act' (VI, 4).

Clearer, more knowledgeable distinctions between interprofessional perspectives and styles signal more confidence and dependability to approach people whom must now be worked with closely in reformed services. In JULIP it is invariably the action learning set meeting that has led to this heightened attunement to sectoral and occupational differences: 'You can pick out influences on the system in the dialogue within the set' (III, 6). From recognizing this in the set, the next step is to coalesce diverse perspectives on the job: 'I'm better [at work] at understanding where people are coming from and putting people's thoughts together' (VI, 5). Not all managers in JULIP of course make this next critical step from set to workplace: 'in practice, joined-up learning is this set, not outside ... We are doing this in the set – [but] not crossing over through the organization' (II, 1).

When differentiation is applied reflexively as heightened awareness of one's own style, does this make the practitioner more sensitive to how they might be seen by others who will look to them for reliance?

> it's about looking at yourself and your organization through another person's eyes ... [refers to important national strategy]: I went along to a meeting ... I was shocked no one else was there from the PCT. But that makes me wonder how others see our Trust's regard for this issue as a priority.
>
> (I, 2)

What difference then do the skills of seeing difference make in practice? Four women managers distinguish below how differentiating across sectors (learning the action learning skill of P in JULIP) helps them join up their work:

First, it helps preview scope to take things forward with the other party: '"How much latitude *do* you have?", I may ask now. Before, I wasn't appreciative of their constraints' (I, 1). It can clarify rules of engagement: 'I understand the rules of the game better, understand the parameters that people have to work in. That helps in bringing that out of people' (I, 2). A third professional appreciates the distinctiveness in reality testing the other sector: 'in dealing with "deadwood": harder in the NHS than in local authorities and social services departments' (IV, 4). Finally, the capacity to differentiate across sectors can more accurately heighten the urgency for cross-sectoral approaches: 'The need for more people to be more flexible in their approach ... getting out of their silos. Be more matrixed in their working ... And JULIP does help us to do this' (II, 3).

How might the structure of action learning actually help people hone their differentiating the kinds of things externalized above through a sharpened skill of P? Within their sets in JULIP, practitioners can dis-identify from the emotional 'swamp' of job pressures felt outside the set. The set allows a companionable sanctuary, a temporary distance from intensive experiencing of work: '[In the set] You could make things less tangible [feel less immersed and in the grip of them]' (VI, 4). A colleague agrees with her: 'In terms of the set, I could be detached from work *and* related to work' (VI, 2). These informants are explaining the cultivation of critical consciousness which enables practitioners to find ways forward with others when unsure what to do next. They are increasing their ability to both participate *and* observe, intervene *and* monitor, engage in particular practice at work *and* reflect on general performance in the set.

With the reflective disengagement and heightened awareness that the set nurtures, deeper-level thinking of experience becomes possible. Secure among colleagues where 'there's no investment in the issue' (I, 3), practitioners can raise fresh questions about performance and strategic implications about change: 'we sat within our own work [in the set] exploring what partnerships meant to us and raising lots and lots of questions that I would have never thought of' (VII, 5).

This exploration 'encourage[s] criticism ... invite[s] criticism' (II, I). Invariably, such supportive scrutiny will turn inward:

> Set meetings also really shaped how I deal with relationships and others.
> Researcher: Can you give an example?
> That this programme forces reflection, sometimes to uncomfortable degrees. For example, I reviewed [in the set] a conflict with a very senior person. It was very helpful: I might have blown it. The set offered a voice of reason, against my voice of passion.
>
> (VI, 4)

Once learning shifts from appreciating external things to be known 'out there' to pursuing less accessible insights 'in here', another key learning skill is in play. Learning about oneself and one's impact on others is less associated with knowledge *about things* (P) and more with *direct experience* – often of people and processes. We are now in another realm of action learning, shifting from the skills of P to those of Q.

ENGAGING TRUST: THE SKILL OF Q IN JOINED UP ACTION LEARNING

> My role [a new post] wasn't thought through – 'partnerships' is a buzz word. Everyone knew there were a number of things to work on, but my role in the PCT was not thought through. So my presence raised expectations [with both prospective and real partners], and I didn't take account of where these 'partners' were coming from [note: in this analysis, the informant was ignorant of P in interdependence]. The set helped me clarify what I wanted to achieve. I checked my expectations [in the set] and found that very helpful
>
> (VI, 1)

When we hear people acknowledge ignorance ('didn't take account of where partners were coming from') and uncertainty (as revealed by the reflective practitioner from the previous section: 'makes me wonder how others see our Trust'), we are witnessing in action learning the emergence of Q, the skill of questioning insight. Learning to engage a relationship built on trust is not merely a matter of increasing P, simply coming to know countless things one ought to trust (the other's professional values or statutory obligations or national frameworks). Trust is an experience of feeling. Learning trust requires more than just understanding what is known about it (Revans was fond of saying, 'P is necessary but insufficient'). Successful experience of taking risks and dealing openly with others in the set in JULIP appears associated with renewed will in joint working outside the set to constructively confront others – demonstrating respect by showing you take them seriously and thereby giving and inviting their trust:

[In work] I am willing to ask the questions and make the challenges. And sitting at PCT level with grassroots perspectives, I'm quite willing to challenge and ask what this really means for the patient. Perhaps I wouldn't have before.

(III, 3)

Indeed, engaging in difficult conversations appears a hallmark of learning Q skills in JULIP, a self-reported area of impact far beyond the action learning set:

I can think of a male colleague in JULIP whom I used to work with. He was asking questions in meetings which are quite challenging which he would have never done before. When I saw this happening, I would say to myself about the person being questioned: 'You're being JULIPed!'

(I, 1)

Can we account for how the will constructively to challenge is strengthened through meeting in a work-focused peer circle? It doesn't happen instantly: '[At first] We were being too nice with each other' (IV, 4). ' ... we needed after a while our set to be more challenging. We were very polite' (I, 2). But gentle beginnings can prepare firmness for later robust exchange:

We then moved to a lot more depth and honesty: 'This is what I want to talk about.' Not 'what we ought to be talking about'.

(VI, 2)

The group has also been there in some tough times. One or two moments when there has been a strong challenge, for example, when [name of colleague in set] said to me, 'Are you running away?'

(V, 1)

Is there evidence that successful challenging (and, also importantly, experience of being successfully challenged) builds confidence outside the set 'to say what needs saying' (I, 2)?

We have all become more open to the idea of exploring issues with other people, and in particular with people not directly involved in that immediate area of work. In fact, feedback would suggest that we all now actively encourage and even organize this outside of our JULIP set.

(II in written note from set)

Here is further reported evidence that this skill of acting more assertively and opening up issues is being transferred beyond the confines of the set of where it is being learnt. One set wrote to the evaluator, 'Our confidence in taking action, in learning and in dealing with "change management" situations, has been developed' (II). At the visit, this theme was expressed by one member as 'out-of-the-box thinking: I feel confident I can do something strange . . .' (II, 2). Her colleague corroborated her own gain in confidence consciously to modify her change-management style outside the set:

> You have to behave differently in different situations and you can't stay the same. You have to change your way of working to achieve different goals. I now try to push for small nuggets that people can get their hands on.
>
> (II, 3)

Again, more self-report evidence of skills learnt within the action learning set being applied outside of it in different circumstances. Renewed confidence underpins the application: the joined up structure of the action learning and research programme has supported 'how confident we are feeling' (IV, 3): 'JULIP has helped me be much more confident in being at the table negotiating these kinds of things . . . The set has been the vehicle' (I, 2). Confidence is always needed in health and social care to talk straight when a blame culture can so easily make a forthright person feel vulnerable. But it may take a year and a dozen set meetings in JULIP before a professional can learn to trust owning outright what the problem might be, especially if a part of it is himself:

> It's only the last two or three set meetings I have begun to feel comfortable in sharing *real* issues bothering me at work, and put these on the table. Offloading: 'This is about *me*.'
> Because I am proud, that's been hard . . . [But] I could carry it back to the set. It was a place you felt *safe*.
>
> (VI, 1)

And what makes a place feel safe?

> Trust: how much you feel able to expose yourself and challenge each other.
>
> (VI, 3)

> We are very honest in our relationship within the set. We do trust each as trustful.
>
> (I, 3)

And so constructive feelings among interorganizational professionals go full circle: trust begetting trust. The study is clear that successful experience of formative trust within the set bolsters functional trust outside it. This finding in JULIP corroborates observations elsewhere: 'Partnership development takes considerable time and those HAZs [Health Action Zones] that have experienced most difficulty are those that have least collective collaborative memory to draw upon' (Barnes and Sullivan 2002: 94). Neurological technology behind emotion science takes the social metaphor further, recognizing how individual bodily memory actually builds capacity to trust through additive reinforcement: 'People who trust a little can gamble and learn to trust more' (Lewis *et al.* 2001: 174).

CONCLUSION

The article has reviewed a *'structure d'acceuil'* – a framework of welcome (Revans 1980: 45) – that creates space in the action learning set for supporting the twin characteristics of interorganizational partnership in the public sector: interdependence and trust. The former – 'Getting right the imperative of customer service' – and the latter – 'with good staff relationships' (IV, 5) – have been seen to be lodged in the forefront of interprofessionals in the study: 'The PCT concentrates on structure [interdependence]; I'm going beyond that to people [trust]' (III, 1). What is found to be less welcoming and more problematic for transferring these skills of openness honed within sets to outside them, however, is the relentless pressure on superiors to manager quantitatively: 'Employers . . . fix on the speed of change and level of monitoring . . . the hard measures' (VI, 2). Their preoccupation to manage upward ironically jeopardizes the relational impact on the very people whose productivity they need to inspire:

> I couldn't explore these [performance problems] with my social services manager if he was in the set.
>
> (II, 3)

> For set members, there's no investment in the issue.
>
> (I, 3)

> it's easier to talk to these people [set colleagues] about it.
>
> (II, 1)

Yet the challenge remains not just to look – and talk – inward: 'in practice, joined up learning is this set, not outside . . . We are doing this in the set – [but] not crossing over through the organization' (II, 1). To transfer learning from set into system requires keeping the meeting 'much more work focused – work related kept it on track' (VI, 2). Some small action steps, with this in mind, were recommended to JULIP's Project Team to further the synergy between what practitioners were finding through their action learning and research and what they were disseminating as models of good interorganizational practice to their employers (Mann 2003b).

The study has presented self-reported evidence that joined up action learning and research in JULIP does support new behaviour in changing things beyond the set: 'Finding ways you *can* do things rather than interpreting rules conservatively' (II, 1 – and this from the inward looking set above). For others, the support from JULIP for joint working has influenced career attitudes:

We are in a culture that wants instant results ... If we are going to make a difference, it will take a longer time.

Researcher: How would you make a difference?

I just felt, when I started, 'That's their problem.' But it's no good saying that ... Writing and reflecting and being in sets and studying makes me think what relationship I am going to make that will make a difference. It's up to me. Won't happen by itself.

(II, 3)

For some, the support from JULIP has left a deeper mark: 'It changed the way I look at the world: being more open and having more perspectives and questioning more' (III, 2). It can be very deep, as one wrote:

The most significant change is that I now feel a new zest for life, a desire to explore the unknown and an ability to see things through the eyes of others. I used to shy away from the conflicts that so often emerge through the complex systems and web of relationships that I work in ... Embracing 'differentness' and celebrating the learning from 'walking in the shoes of others' is part of whom I have become through studying for the Masters. I have come to realize that only then can you get the different perspective and begin to create a whole picture ...

My 'Aha' moment came almost a year after starting the journey. I was at a learning set meeting ... I talked for the first time about having options, new doors were opening, and I had made a cognitive shift from believing that I was powerless to being empowered. As one of my colleagues in the learning set said at the time, 'I am now getting a sense of you in all of this.' The integration of self had started ...

(VII, 5 in written note to researcher)

The study has depicted the link between achieving the soft variable of relational trust as a prerequisite to addressing the hard variable of functional interdependence. Action learning and research in JULIP does prime successful experience of the first variable: 'in the set you can really concentrate on and challenge in depth somebody's issue' (I, 3) and rely on them to 'really question what you are doing' (VII, 5). And this renewed individual confidence supports practitioners' tackling the second outside the set, doggedly pursuing 'What questions do we need to be answering?' (I, 2). It is the set which structures the space for seamlessly joining professional with personal, rational with emotional. Recent studies in change leadership acknowledge 'links to neurology' (Goleman *et al.* 2002) in human change capacity whereby 'Speaking to people's feelings ... not just thoughts' influences their trust of others by going 'deeper than the conscious and analytic part of our brains' (Kotter and Cohen 2002: x and 182). Is action learning reaching the part of the brain that taught coursework doesn't? Do set meetings orchestrate limbic resonance – that 'symphony of mutual exchange and internal adaptation' through which today's interorganizational professionals 'become attuned to each other's inner states' (Lewis *et al.* 2001: 63)?

REFERENCES

Asthana, S., Richardson, S. and Halliday, J. (2002) 'Partnership Working in Public Policy Provision: A Framework for Evaluation'. *Social Policy and Administration*, 36:7 pp780–95.

Attwood, M. (1994) 'Developing Organisations across Boundaries'. Briefing Paper, NHS Training Directorate.

Attwood, M., Pedler, M., Pritchard, S. and Wilkinson, D. (2003) *Leading Change – a Guide to Whole Systems Working*, Bristol: The Policy Press.

Audit Commission (1998) *A Fruitful Partnership: Effective Partnership Working*, London: Audit Commission.

Balloch, S. and Taylor, M. eds (2001) *Partnership Working: Policy and Practice*, Bristol: The Policy Press.

Barnes, M. and Sullivan, H. (2002) 'Building Capacity for Collaboration in English Health Action Zones' in C. Glendinning, M. Powell and K. Rummery (eds) *Partnerships, New Labour and the Governance of Welfare*. Bristol: The Policy Press.

Boot, R. and Reynolds, M. (1997) 'Groups, Groupwork and Beyond' in J. Burgoyne and M. Reynolds (eds) *Management Learning*. London: Sage Publications.

Boyne, G., Farrell, C., Law, J., Powell, M. and Walker, R. (2003) *Evaluating Public Management Reforms*, Buckingham: Open University Press.

Bradford, N. (2003) 'Public–Private Partnership? Shifting Paradigms of Economic Governance in Ontario'. *Canadian Journal of Political Science*, 36:5 pp1005–33.

Brown, G. (1973) 'Some Thoughts on Grounded Theory'. *Sociology*, 7 pp1–16.

Burgoyne, J. and Reynolds, M. (1997) *Management Learning*, London: Sage Publications.

Calnan, M. and Gabe, J. (2001) 'From Consumerism to Partnership: Britain's National Health Service at the Turn of the Century'. *International Journal of Health Services*, 31:1 pp119–31.

Cameron, A. and Lart, R. (2003) 'Factors Promoting and Obstacles Hindering Joint Working: A Systematic Review of the Research Evidence'. *Journal of Integrated Care*, 11:2 pp9–17.

Clarke, J. and Glendinning, C. (2002) 'Partnership and the Remaking of Welfare Governance' in C. Glendinning, M. Powell and K. Rummery (eds) *Partnerships, New Labour and the Governance of Welfare*. Bristol: The Policy Press.

Coleman, A. and Rummery, K. (2003) 'Social Services Representation in Primary Care Groups and Trusts'. *Journal of Interprofessional Care*, 17:3 pp273–81.

Collins, H. (1979) 'The Investigation of Frames of Meaning: Complementarity and Compromise'. *Sociological Review*, 27:4 pp703–18.

Considine, M. and Lewis, J. (2003) 'Networks and Interactivity: Making Sense of Front-Line Governance in the United Kingdom, the Netherlands and Australia'. *Journal of European Public Policy*, 10:1 pp46–58.

Cooper, R. and Sawaf, A. (1998) *Executive EQ: Emotional Intelligence in Business*, London: Orion Business Books.

Coppel, D. and Dyas, J. (2003) 'Strengthening Links between Health Action Zone Evaluation and Primary Care Research'. *Primary Health Care Research and Development*, 4:1 pp39–47.

Craig, G., Taylor, M., Wilkinson, M. Monro, S. Bloor, K. and Syed, A. (2002) *Contract or Trust? The Role of Compacts in Local Governance*, Bristol: The Policy Press.

Dixon, N. (2000) *Common Knowledge*, Boston, MA: Harvard Business School Press.

Drake, K. (1995) 'The Economics of Learning on the Job: A European Perspective on Instruction-Led and Experience-Led Job Competence'. *Efficiency and Equity in Education Policy*, proceedings of a conference convened by the National Board of Employment, Education and Training in association with the Centre for Economic Policy Research, Australian National University, Canberra, Australian Government Publishing Service

Evaluation Buzz Group Report to Project Team (2003) Unpublished internal note to Project Team, 27 January.

Geddes, M. and Benington, J. eds (2001) *Local Partnerships and Social Exclusion in the European Union: New Forms of Local Social Governance?*, London: Routledge.

Giddens, A. (1998) *The Third Way: The Renewal of Social Democracy*, Cambridge: Polity Press.

Glaser, B. (1978) *Theoretical Sensitivity: Advances in the Methodology of Grounded Theory*, Mill Valley, CA: The Sociology Press.

Glendinning, C., Abbott, S. and Coleman, A. (2001) 'Bridging the Gap: New Relationships between Primary Care Groups and Local Authorities'. *Social Policy and Administration*, 35:4 pp411–25.

Glendinning, C., Powell, M. and Rummery, K. eds (2002) *Partnerships, New Labour and the Governance of Welfare*, Bristol: The Policy Press.

Goleman, D. (1996) *Emotional Intelligence: Why It Can Matter More Than IQ*, London: Bloomsbury.

Goleman, D., Boyatzis, R. and McKee, A. (2002) *The New Leaders: Transforming the Art of Leadership into the Science of Results*, London: Little, Brown.

Harrison, S. and Dowswell, G. (2002) 'Autonomy and Bureaucratic Accountability in Primary Care'. *Sociology of Health and Illness*, 24:2 pp208–26.

Hudson, B. (2000) 'Social Services and Primary Care Groups: A Window of Collaborative Opportunity?'. *Health and Social Care in the Community*, 8:4 pp242–50.

Hudson, B., Hardy, B., Henwood, M. and Wistow, G. (1997) 'Working across Professional Boundaries: Primary Health Care and Social Care'. *Public Money and Management*, 17:4 pp25–30.

Huxham, C. (2000) 'The Challenge of Collaborative Governance'. *Public Management*, 2:3 pp337–57.

Jessop, B. (2000) 'Governance Failure' in B. Stoker (ed.) *The New Politics of British Urban Governance*. Basingstoke: Macmillan.

Jupp, B. (2000) *Working Together*, London: Demos.

Kotter, J. and Cohen, D. (2002) *The Heart of Change: Real Life Stories of How People Change Their Organizations*, Boston, MA: Harvard Business School Press.

Lewin, R. and Regine, B. (1999) *The Soul at Work: Unleashing the Power of Complexity Science for Business Success*, London: Orion Business Book.

Lewis, T., Amini, F. and Lannon, R. (2001) *A General Theory of Love*, New York: Vintage.

Ling, T. (2002) 'Delivering Joined-Up Government in the UK: Dimensions, Issues and Problems'. *Public Administration*, 80:4 pp615–42.

Locke, K. (2001) *Grounded Theory in Management Research*, London: Sage Publications.

Mann, P. (1999) 'Can We Make Development Training Developmental?'. *Public Administration and Development*, 19:1 pp105–16.

——— (2003a) 'Evaluation of JULIP: Some Initial Expectations of the Evaluator'. Unpublished note to the Project Team, 23 March.

——— (2003b) 'JULIP: Joined Up Learning in Partnership: A Progress Report'. Unpublished 42-page study for Project Team, 12 October.

Miller, C. and Ahmad, Y. (2000) 'Collaboration and Partnership: An Effective Response to Complexity and Fragmentation or Solution Built on Sand?'. *International Journal of Sociology and Social Policy*, 20:5 pp1–38.

Morgan, G. (1986) *Images of Organization*, Newbury Park, CA: Sage Publications.

Morris, J. (1987) 'Good Company'. *Management Education and Development*, 18:2 pp103–15.

Newman, J. (2001) *Modernising Governance: New Labour, Policy and Society*, London: Sage Publications.

NHS Management Executive (NHSME) (1991) 'A Management Development Strategy for the NHS'. Leeds: NHS Training Directorate.

Nonaka, I. and Takeuchi, H. (1995) *The Knowledge-Creating Company*, New York: OUP.

Ovretveit, J. (2003) 'Nordic Privatization and Private Healthcare'. *International Journal of Health Planning and Management*, 18:3 pp233–46.

Papadopoulos, Y. (2003) 'Cooperative Forms of Governance: Problems of Democratic Accountability in Complex Environments'. *European Journal of Political Research*, 42:4 pp473–501.

Partlett, M. and Hamilton, D. (1972) 'Evaluation as Illumination: A New Approach to the Study of Innovatory Programs'. Occasional Paper (University of Edinburgh, Centre for Research in the Education Sciences), October.

Paton, C. (1999) 'New Labour's Health Policy' in M. Powell (ed.) *New Labour, New Welfare State?* Bristol: The Policy Press.

Pedler, M. (1997) 'Interpreting Action Learning' in J. Burgoyne and M. Reynolds (eds) *Management Learning*. London: Sage Publications.

Pedler, M., Burgoyne, J. and Boydell, T. (1991) *The Learning Company: A Strategy for Sustainable Development*, Maidenhead: McGraw-Hill.

Pettigrew, P. (2003) 'Power, Conflicts and Resolutions: A Change Agent's Perspective on Conducting Action Research within a Multiorganizational Partnership'. *Systematic Practice and Action Research*, 16:6 pp375–91.

Powell, M. ed. (1999) *New Labour, New Welfare State?*, Bristol: The Policy Press.

Powell, M. and Exworthy, M. (2002) 'Partnerships, Quasi-Networks and Social Policy' in C. Glendinning, M. Powell and K. Rummery (eds) *Partnerships, New Labour and the Governance of Welfare*. Bristol: The Policy Press.

Pritchard, S. (2003) 'Report on the Pilot Learning Groups for Children and Families and Mental Health Teams'. Unpublished, Royal Borough of Kensington and Chelsea.

Revans, R. (1980) *Action Learning: New Techniques for Management*, London: Blond & Briggs.
——— (1982) *The Origins and Growth of Action Learning*, Bromley: Chartwell Bratt.
——— (1983) *The ABC of Action Learning*, Bromley: Chartwell Bratt.

Rhodes, R. (1997) *Understanding Governance*, Buckingham: Open University Press.

Rummery, K. (2002) 'Towards a Theory of Welfare Partnerships' in C. Glendinning, M. Powell and K. Rummery (eds) *Partnerships, New Labour and the Governance of Welfare*. Bristol: The Policy Press.
——— (2004) 'Progress towards Partnership? The Development of Relations between Primary Care Organisations Social Services Concerning Older People's Services in the UK'. *Social Policy and Society*, 3:1 (forthcoming).

Rummery, K. and Coleman, A. (2003) 'Primary Health and Social Care Services in the UK: Progress towards Partnership?'. *Social Science and Medicine*, 56:8 pp1773–82.

Secretary of State for Health (1997) *The New NHS: Modern, Dependable*, Cm3807, London: The Stationery Office.
——— (2000) *The NHS Plan*, Cm4818, London: The Stationery Office.

Senge, P. (1990) *The Fifth Discipline: The Art and Practice of the Learning Organisation*, London: Random House.

Spencer, L. and Dale, A. (1979) 'Integration and Regulation in Organizations: A Contextual Approach'. *Sociological Review*, 27:4 pp679–702.

Stoker, G. (2000) 'Urban Political Science and the Challenge of Urban Governance' in J. Pierre (ed.) *Debating Governance: Authority, Steering and Democracy*. Oxford: Oxford University Press.

Sullivan, H. and Skelcher, C. (2002) *Working across Boundaries*, Basingstoke: Palgrave.

Vince, R. and Martin, L. (1993) 'Inside Action Learning: An Exploration of the Psychology and Politics of the Action Learning Model'. *Management Education and Development*, 24:3 pp205–15.

Weiland, G. and Bradford, A. (1981) 'An Evaluation of the Hospital Internal Communications Project' in *Improving Health Care Management*. Ann Arbor, MI: Health Administration Press.

Zimmerman, B., Lindberg, C. and Plsek, P. (1998) *Edgeware: Lessons from Complexity Science for Health Care Leaders*, Dallas, TX: VHA.

Zohar, D. and Marshall, I. (2000) *Spiritual Intelligence: The Ultimate Intelligence*, London: Bloomsbury.

NOTES ON CONTRIBUTORS

Kerry Brown is the Director of the Work and Industry Futures Research Program in the Faculty of Business, Queensland University of Technology. She is a Senior Lecturer in the School of Management and her research interests include public sector organizations, culture change and industrial relations.

Reginald Butterfield is the managing director of Management Resource Centre (MRC), an organizational and management development consultancy working throughout Europe. He has over 35 years public/private sector business, academic and consultancy experience. Reg gained his MBA and Ph.D. at Kingston University, England. Reg has been a member of the UK Chartered Management Institute since 1992.

Christine Edwards is the Head of School for HRM at Kingston Business School. She has researched and published in the field of management and flexible working in the public sector.

Dianne Lewis is an Adjunct Professor of Management at the Queensland University of Technology, Brisbane, Australia. She researches and publishes widely in the areas of organizational culture, change and leadership and has extensive experience in the analysis of documentation providing insights into corporate culture. Professor Lewis specializes in the study of public sector and not-for-profit organizations and in both her research and consultancy she has had experience in analysing these types of organizations structurally, culturally and strategically with the aim of helping them plan for the future.

Marilyn McDougall is an independent academic and consultant. She is Visiting Professor of Human Resource Development at Glasgow Caledonian University, and in addition to work–life balance, has research interests in executive development processes particularly mentoring and coaching.

Pete Mann works in the Institute for Development Policy and Management (IDPM) which – with effect from September 2004 – is in the new School of Environment and Development at the new University of Manchester. He is keen on the development of practice and how learningful working environments can be engendered during intensive times of organizational change. His interests span action learning, accounting for one's own practice and body–mind psychology.

Gillian Maxwell is a senior lecturer in human resource management. Her research interests and publications centre on strategic human resource issues and developments, for example diversity and quality service. Current research projects in which she is involved include work–life balance and gender balance in management.

Philippe Méhaut is an economist, a director of research at the Laboratory for Labour Economics and Industrial Sociology in Aix en Provence. His main fields of research include school-to-work transition, further education and training at micro or macro levels, including international comparisons.

Coralie Perez is an economist, researcher at the Center of Research on Qualifications (Cereq) in Marseille. Her fields of research include further education and training and the evaluation of public and private policies.

Sue Pritchard is Chair of Monmouthshire Local Health Board and, at the time of writing, was Visiting Research Fellow at the Revans Institute for Action Learning and Research. She has been an independent consultant in management and organization learning for some thirteen years, with a strong interest in 'whole system' development. Sue has supported the London-based multi-organization partnership project called 'Julip' since its conception in 1997.

John J. Rodwell is an Associate Professor at the Macquarie Graduate School of Management, Macquarie University. He recently returned to academia after a spell as head of analytics at Lloyds TSB Bank plc in London. John specializes in knowledge management, strategic human resource management, call/contact centre management and organizational behaviour. John has successfully conducted consultancy projects for more than fourteen years on issues ranging from employee surveys, job stress diagnostics, HRM practices and brand management training for senior product managers, through to knowledge management, customer relationship management and data mining. John's current research emphasis within knowledge management is on the integration of management and marketing practices within a knowledge management context, with strategic HRM as a key means of generating human capital.

Kirstein Rummery is a lecturer in Social Policy in the School of Social Sciences at the University of Manchester. She has worked previously at the Universities of Birmingham and Kent, and she has researched and published in the area of community care, disability rights, partnership working between primary health and social care and governance of the welfare state.

Stephen T. T. Teo is currently a Senior Lecturer in Human Resource Management at the University of Technology Sydney, after ten years working in the Malaysian and Australian banking industries. Stephen has researched and published in the fields of strategic HRM, international HRM and social network analysis. His doctoral research examined the effectiveness of the corporate HR department of a public sector entity during commercialization. Stephen's research interests include strategic HRM and Chinese business networks in the Asia-Pacific.

Jennifer Waterhouse is a Post-Doctoral Fellow at the School of Management, Queensland University of Technology, Brisbane, Australia. She is a member of the Work and Industry Futures Research Concentration in the Faculty of Business. Her research interests include public sector management, employment relations and organizational communication, culture and change.

Jean Woodall is Associate Dean and Professor of HRD at Business School at Oxford Brooks University. She is also the current Editor-in-Chief of *Human Resource Development International*. She has co-edited *New Frontiers in HRD* with Monica Lee and Jim Stewart (Routledge, 2004) and *Ethical Issues in Contemporary Human Resource Development* (Palgrave, 2000) with Diana Winstanley, with whom she also co-authored *Management Development: Strategy and Practice* (Blackwell, 1998). She has published articles on a wide range of topics including, career management for women, work-related management development, ethics and HRD, HRD outsourcing and professional learning.

Index: Human Resource Management in the Public Sector (Beattie and Osborne)

ʰe United Kingdom by
ʳce UK Ltd., Milton Keynes
ᵇB/289-291/P

9 780415 464253